The Daughters of Danu

The Daughters of Danu

Piet Ceanadach

MOON
BOOKS

Winchester, UK
Washington, USA

First published by Moon Books, 2011
Moon Books is an imprint of John Hunt Publishing Ltd., Laurel House, Station Approach,
Alresford, Hants, SO24 9JH, UK
office1@o-books.net
www.o-books.com

For distributor details and how to order please visit the 'Ordering' section on our website.

Text copyright: Piet Ceanadach 2010

ISBN: 978 1 84694 614 1

A CIP catalogue record for this book is available from the British Library.

Design: Stuart Davies

Printed in the UK by CPI Antony Rowe
Printed in the USA by Offset Paperback Mfrs, Inc

We operate a distinctive and ethical publishing philosophy in all
areas of our business, from our global network of authors to
production and worldwide distribution.

CONTENTS

Rainfall

Book One

In the Village of the Salmon

My name is Orla. I have lived in this village from the day I was born, fifteen summers ago.

I've just been woken by the constant sound of rain. It feels like it's been raining for months but in reality it's probably only been a few weeks. It's not very light outside, in fact, it's a miserable grey colour so I reckon it's still fairly early, but it's hard to tell when the clouds above are so black and heavy with rain, even the animals are quiet. The bad weather is getting to everyone even the beasts.

My father, Branan the village black smith, is worried that the village crops will be ruined if this awful weather doesn't improve. He says that if it goes on much longer, every man, woman and child will have to go out into the fields and gather in what we can save. He says that if the weather doesn't get any better there won't be enough food to carry us through the winter. In the blessed name of Danu I hope he is wrong.

It's nice and warm under this fur snuggled in with my little sister Sorcha, warming my back. Still, I am aware of my responsibilities and must get up and help my mother make something to eat. It's still hard to get up though. My father, normally the first to rise, will soon return from tending the smithy fire and he will be hungry. Sorcha stirs as I gently slide from under the furs, she groans at being disturbed but soon settles down again, slipping back into the steady rhythm of sleep.

"Gràinne," my father whispered as he entered dripping into the house shaking the rain from his cloak, "I think the village animals are more depressed than we are." My father was always one for a joke, but this time even she found it difficult to force even a wry smile.

"Come Branan, sit and have some breakfast, I'll wake little Sorcha, it's time she was up". "Orla dear, build up the hearth, let's keep the damp out or we'll all be ill."

"That's my mother, always the practical one," I said inwardly. She looked over at me, winked, ran her fingers through her auburn curls and went to wake Sorcha.

Over breakfast my father announced that all the villagers would be meeting in the great hall to consider what is to be done before all of our harvest is ruined.

"Are we all going father," I asked inquisitively.

"Yes," he said, "If we work together we will achieve more."

I nodded showing I understood. He looked up from his breakfast bowl and smiled approvingly.

"Do I have to go father," chirped Sorcha, "I don't like the rain and it's cold."

"Oh, I'll carry you under my cloak, that way you won't get your lovely red hair wet," father laughed, but I could see in his eyes he was worried.

We quickly tidied up and dressed into our waterproof sealskins. I ran a bone comb through my long chestnut coloured hair, and as a family we crossed the small village of seventeen round houses to the larger meetinghouse as the rain continued to fall.

Once inside I naturally looked around to see who was there. The hearth had been built up, it was cosy but a little smoky, old men coughed and children rubbed their irritated eyes. My father sat at the head of the circle with the other village elders, Fionn and Rónan, the druid Cathal sat nearby and I peeped out nosily watching the rain through the crack in the door cover. At first I thought I saw someone across the clearing, but when I looked again they were gone. I put it down to the blur of the smoke and the persistent rain falling. My attention was drawn back to the gathering as Cathal hushed everybody to silence, and then in his usual orderly way, he invited all the men and women in turn to voice their opinions as to what was to be done. Cathal briefly emphasised the urgency of the situation and turning to his left nodded to indicate that Una, Niall's wife should start the discussion. After Niall in came Mòrag, followed by her man Taran. And so one after the other all had their say.

"Orla my dear, do you have any thoughts?" Enquired Cathal.

"Lord Druid," I nervously replied, being surprised at being included "I am only 15 summers old."

Cathal looked me in the eye and said, "You have grown so quickly Orla, and I do not think that any who are here would not value your opinion." "Speak and tell us what your thoughts are?"

I could see my mother and father looking startled at me, and it made me nervous.

"I think," I stuttered, "Danu will help us, Perhaps if we wait a few more days the rain will stop and that will give us the opportunity to bring in our crops," I enthused unconvincingly.

Niall shook his head, and looking directly at me said,

"If we wait too long we will lose everything Orla."

Taran, Morag and Rónan all nodded in agreement. There was a great murmur in the hall and even the children felt the unrest that had been stirred.

"Cathal, why ask the opinion of a child," sneered Fionn, looking over at me, and obviously frustrated by what he considered to be a complete waste of time.

Cathal feeling a rise in the temperature rose to his feet and held his arms open wide, palms open. "Peace my people, this is not a time for anger, but a time to cooperate".

"If we continue to wait for the intervention of the Gods, we'll probably all starve to death in our houses, tell me, who has seen or felt the touch of the old ones in our lifetime?" Snapped Fionn, with a great deal of frustration in his voice. "They're just stories we tell our children," he mumbled as he rose to his feet to leave.

Some nodded in agreement; others let it go as the frustrations of a worried man. When Fionn realised that the Druid had not closed the meeting, he sat back down again, not wishing to insult those present, for in our times it was considered good manners to remain seated during a meeting. Cathal stepped closer to the hearth fire; the lines on his face could be clearly seen. He spoke of togetherness and cooperation, looking at each person including the little ones as he spoke in a vain attempt to hide his concern. Letting out a deep breath, he thanked everyone for their solidarity, even Fionn who was still shaking his head and muttering through his teeth, and ended the meeting of the villagers. Only my father Branan, Rónan and a rather vexed Fionn stayed behind to plan the ingathering.

As the sun dipped down low in the watery sky my father came home.

"It is agreed that we should wait until the third daybreak from today, which will allow us time to plan who does what and when, Gràinne, do we have any mead left, my bones are like ice?" My father said suddenly.

"Er, I think so Branan, are you feeling ill?"

Father looked across at Gràinne and said, "No, just cold, but I think it's time for a toast. Orla, I was proud of you today, Cathal agreed with you that we should wait a short while, let's hope it's to our advantage."

I just smiled and looked across at Sorcha, who playfully stuck her tongue out at me.

Sorcha and I set out the food and left mother and father to talk together. Although I couldn't hear what they were saying, I could feel the worry in the atmosphere, but I thought it best if I kept quiet.

I started to daydream about the gathering and my mind suddenly reminded me of the figure I thought I saw outside across the clearing through the rain. I tried to picture the shape and I conclude that it looked like a man in a green cloak, although I wasn't absolutely sure. Just as I decided not to mention the incident, somebody tapped on the doorframe.

"Orla, can you get that," my mother said softly.

"Okay," I replied, walking to the door expecting to see a familiar face. Like most girls of my age when faced with a stranger, especially a man, I stumbled over my words. "Er, c-can I help you?". The young man looked back at me and gave me a reassuring look.

"My name is Eóghann, I'm from a village to the west of here and I'm travelling to visit my kin, is it possible to find a little food and shelter here in your village, the weather is very bad for travelling?"

At that moment my father who had heard a male voice came to the door and saved my blushes.

"Hello young man, what can we do for you"? My father enquired. Eóghann repeated his request, and my father turned to my mother who by now was standing right behind him and asked if we could stretch what we had for a guest. Eóghann was welcomed over our doorstep and he took off his green topcoat. I couldn't help notice that Eóghann wasn't all that wet, in fact his hair was almost dry and his boots, the like I've never seen before, were still bright and shiny.

"Have you come far?" Enquired my mother as she gave him a bowl of steaming hot broth and a piece of bread.

"Just beyond the isles out to the west," he said as he sipped at the broth.

"Ah!" Said my father, "That accounts for your accent, I guess."

"Yes Branan, that is probably the reason," Eóghann replied quietly into his bowl.

I think because everybody else was busying themselves, I was the only one to hear what Eóghann had said.

"How did he know my father's name?" I thought. Eóghann looked across at me and smiled.

"By the Gods and Goddesses he can hear my thoughts," I

reasoned uncomfortably.

This time Eóghann didn't look up but continued to eat his meal. I settled down a little then and put all thoughts of a 'mind reader' out of my head, but not completely. Sorcha intrigued by a stranger in our home wanted naturally to sit next to him.

"Please, please, please can I sit next to – "Eóghann is my name Sorcha," he said in an almost musical tone.

"He's done it again," I thought. This time Eóghann did look up. And it was then that I noticed his eyes. His eyes shone like gemstones, there was water and fire, air and earth deep within those eyes and I couldn't help wondering if he was 'otherworldly'.

"Orla" he whispered, "I will help you."

Father came and sat down opposite Eóghann. Mother passed him a bowl of broth and then came and sat next to father.

"Have you been badly affected by the weather in this village?" enquired Eóghann.

"You know we have," I thought, perhaps a little too sharply.

Eóghann looked me directly in the eye chastising me with a glance, I turned away quickly, and turning back to my father listened as Branan my father explained the situation.

"Perhaps I can help, the more able hands you have the quicker the work will be completed," said Eóghann with a very reassuring voice.

"If you can spare the time, we don't wish to keep you from your kin," my father said taken aback by the offer.

"Then if that's all right with you Gràinne, I'll put my things in the smithy."

"Orla, will you show me where I might sleep?" Smiled Eóghann, who rose to his feet and lifted his bag.

"I don't remember that bag," I thought. "I'm sure he came in without a bag."

"Can I come too," cried Sorcha.

"Stay here little one, it's still raining out there, you can go later if the rain stops," father butted in optimistically.

"Orla, don't be long," said my mother like a protective hen watching over her chick.

Once inside the smithy I showed Eóghann the small hayloft that had been built above the noisy animal stalls and fire.

"This is perfect," smiled Eóghann, as he laid his things out on the hay in an orderly fashion.

I was still a little nervous in his company and he knew it.

"Orla, you have no need to worry, I am no threat to you or your family," he said reassuringly, and for some unexplained reason I felt at ease. I was just about to leave when he asked, "Do you believe that if you ask for something good it will be given?"

"I, I don't understand," I babbled nervously.

"Do you think that the 'Old Ones' listen when we talk to them?" He asked softly as he looked me straight in the eye as if he was searching my very soul.

"I know they do," I responded. I stared at him what must have seemed like an eternity. "Who are you Eóghann, you ask the strangest questions, one minute I feel comfortable in your company, the next, apprehensive, what is it that you want?"

Eóghann sat down next to the anvil.

"I've come to help," he smiled that twinkling smile. I swear I saw sunshine in his eyes as he turned to look at the rain clouds passing by the entrance.

"Orla, will you help me make some corn dollies and sun wheels tomorrow, perhaps Sorcha could help too?"

"Er, yes, if that's what you want to do," I responded. I thought he was just trying to divert our minds off the weather and the difficult days to come.

"See you tomorrow then Orla," and just as I was about to leave he said, "And may the lady of the white waters bring you and your people peace and happiness." With those thoughts tumbling around my confused head I returned to our house.

"Orla, is Eóghann comfortable in the smithy?"

"Yes mother he's fine," I responded.

"Father, Eóghann has asked if Sorcha and I can help him make some corn dollies tomorrow. Is that okay?"

Father turned and smiling said, "There's not much happening here for a day or two, it will help occupy your sister for a while, sure you can."

That night we all retired to our beds fairly early. Sorcha was exhausted and soon fell asleep. I could hear mother and father chatting quietly. I didn't mean to eves drop, but when you all sleep in the same room you hear everything. I could hear mother discussing the meeting that was held earlier, and how proud she was that I had spoke so eloquently, and how angry she became when Fionn was dismissive of my opinion. Father kind of grunted his agreement, his mind full of issues. Then the conversation changed, both lowered their voices to a whisper unsure as to whether I was awake or not, unfortunately for them I could still hear what they were saying. My father was whispering that there was something strange about Eóghann; he kind of reminds him of someone, he just can't think whom. Mother sighed, kissed him and said, "Goodnight Branan." Then there was silence and we slept.

I woke to the sound of Sorcha chattering in her sleep, it was still dark. I turned on to my back as my eyes adjusted to what little light came into the room from the outside. I listened, as you do, to the various noises of the night, I could hear in the distance the hooting of an Owl on the hunt. There were scurrying also, rodents perhaps and of course the unwelcome sound of the persistent rainfall. I eased myself out of our cot, trying not to disturb Sorcha and quickly put some clothes on. Tip toeing to the door I very gently lifted the latch and slipped silently out into the cold night air. The shock of the cold made me shiver and I pulled my warm cloak tightly about myself. Just as I was about to step out from the shadows, a vixen came out of the smithy, sniffed the air, looked in my direction, appeared to nod in recognition, and disappeared into the trees at the point just beyond the compound. Now this may seem impossible to you as it did for me, for there is a fence just beyond the smithy but I know what I saw. Like any other inquisitive teenager I wanted to investigate what I had just seen. So, I quietly moved across the compound to find the hole in the fence just beyond the smithy. There wasn't one. Worrying more about being caught outside and having to explain myself, I turned to go back to the house when I noticed a dim light coming from the inside of the smithy. I just had to look, didn't I? Approaching the door as quiet as a mouse I put my hand on the latch and the light instantly went out, startling me, forcing me to step backwards.

"You shouldn't be out in the rain Orla, you'll make yourself ill," came a voice from behind me.

The air rushed out of my lungs as I spun to face the voice, but before I could speak a finger gently touched my lips and Eóghann stepped forward.

"The dawn will break soon Orla, go back to your bed and rest, we have things to do on the morrow."

Without another word passing between us, I backed away and still shaking, turned, and headed quietly, yet quickly towards the house. I slipped silently in through the door and hung my cloak on the hook near my cot, and then I noticed. My cloak was dry, my shoes were dry, and I was dry. "How can this be?" I thought. I tiptoed to the window and lifted the flap; it was still raining.

"Orla, is that you?" "Yes mother, I'm just a little restless, I'm going back to my bed now, goodnight."

"Goodnight dear, goodnight."

Cathal the Druid

It was a long hazardous walk to the Isle of the Druids, but Cathal needed help and advice if he was to be of any help to his people. Although Cathal was a man of many summers, he personally felt that too many hard winters had aged him, having said that, he was still a sprightly man – for his age that is.

Several days after leaving the village of the salmon, it was called that because salmon could be seen yearly migrating up and down the river nearby, Cathal approached the rocky shoreline opposite the Isle of the Druids. Squatting there besides a round boat was a small man who had been blind from birth.

"Cathal, I've been waiting for you," said the blind man with a confident delivery.

"How did you know it was me?" questioned Cathal, with an air of no surprise.

"Everyone has a different gait and I remember yours," mused the boatman quite nonchalantly. "You remember faces, and I remember gaits, it's easy when you don't have the distractions of sight."

Cathal laughed seeing the humour in the boatman's expression. "How did you know I was coming?" smiled Cathal, "No don't insult me with an answer, it was foolish of me to ask."

The boatman chuckled under his breath and said, "We'd better get off then, don't wish to keep anybody waiting, don't you think?"

They both stepped into the coracle and the boatman started to draw strongly on the oars. Cathal watched in absolute amazement as the boatman manoeuvred the little craft in the direction of the Isle. Once away from the shoreline the waters foamed angrily and became quite choppy. The rain hadn't abated.

"Don't worry about a few waves Cathal, it's not your time

yet," puffed the boatman.

Cathal clung to the small craft as if his very life depended on it, regardless of what the boatman had said, little did he know then, but lots of things depended on old Cathal's life. With the wind lifting spray and the constant rocking of the little craft Cathal was glad that his stomach was empty.

The boatman continued to draw on the oars, "Not long now Cathal; not long now."

Cathal wiped the salty seawater from his stinging eyes, and thought, perhaps imagining that the blind boatman didn't appear wet at all.

"Boats and Druids don't do well together, the relentless movement scrambles the senses," thought the Druid.

At the time that the watery sun began his descent towards the grey sea in the west, Cathal the Druid stood on the shore, relieved to have his shaky feet back on solid ground. Cathal looked up where the settlement was and eyeing his direction, took his first stumbling step to leave the shoreline and make his way up the steep incline that led to the settlement. Turning again toward the shore, he was about to thank the blind boatman but he was gone, leaving behind only the sound of the sea, the whisper of the wind, and the cry of the seagulls.

At the top of the slippery path Cathal stood before the familiar door of the settlement that housed the Druid High Counsel. How the time had flown since he, as a young boy, had first entered this place all those seasons ago.

"Cathal my old friend, how good it is to see you again after all this time," came a recognisable voice from the door crack.

Standing before the old Druid stood a short woman with striking features and long grey hair, dressed in the customary blue of one of high rank.

"Ceana, it is wonderful to be in your presence again," bowed Cathal.

"Come in man, don't just stand there passing pleasantries,

there's a warm fire in the hearth if you're interested," Ceana chirped, holding the door open to let Cathal through.

After Ceana had closed the door, she slipped her arm in Cathal's and, arm in arm they walked slowly through the settlement and into the roundhouse.

"Fetch some dry clothes for our guest," beckoned Ceana to a young man who was tending the hearth, "And when you're dry and warm, we will eat together and then we can talk."

Cathal shivered and nodded in total agreement.

Ciaran, a man unknown to Cathal slipped away to gather together the things that Ceana had ordered.

"Ciaran is a good man Cathal," said Ceana as she saw Cathal's gaze follow the young man through the door.

"How long has he been here?"

"About fourteen full seasons, he's a very good student Cathal, he reminds me of you when you were young." Cathal looked over and smiled.

"You've not lost any of your charm then Ceana." A chuckle broke out between them just as Ciaran came through the door with his arms full of clean dry clothes. Ciaran held the dry robe up to the fire to take the chill off it as the old Druid let his damp clothes slide to the floor. "You've lost a little weight my friend, I remember you being bigger than that," winked Ceana, as Cathal stood naked before the fire.

"It's a trick of the firelight, besides it's cold outside and men's bodies react to the cold, didn't you know?" grumbled Cathal, becoming embarrassed at the fun being directed at him.

"Sit down and we'll eat, then you can tell me why your here." Cathal observed a change in Ceana's tone, the small talk was over, and it was now time for counsel.

Ciaran brought in six bowls of steaming broth, setting then out around the hearth, and taking one for himself he stepped just out of earshot and seated himself on a musicians stool and began to play a most beautifully crafted cláirseach. At that moment, as if on key, three other Druids strode into the room taking their places around the hearth. Cathal knew all three, Oisian had been a fellow student with him, and Coinneach and Brighde were his teachers all those seasons ago.

"It's good to see you again," said Cathal, breaking the lull.

"We've been expecting you for some time," came the response.

Cathal didn't say anything else, just a friendly nod, and then he lifted his broth bowl and ate his fill. If nothing else, this short interlude gave him time to gather his thoughts and compose himself. Looking up from his broth he noticed that the others were watching him, as if searching his soul for answers.

"Is there a problem?" Questioned Cathal.

"Not with you Cathal, not with you." Answered Coinneach.

Seeing that Cathal shifted uncomfortably, Ceana rose to her feet, and holding her arms out with her hands open she began, "Cathal old friend, the land is in turmoil and the responsibility is with the High King, what we are to do about it we do not know, but now that you are here, perhaps the answer will be forthcoming."

Francach

In Halls of the High King

King Fionntan had in the past been a good king, but as time went by he had become surrounded by greedy, selfish counsellors, men and women who corrupted his mind, and more importantly, his heart. After his wife became ill and took to her sickbed, King Fionntan found comfort in the arms of others who were more than willing to manipulate the old King for what they could. Sadly, the old King had also forgotten his other marriage, that of the land. It is written, that in the old law of Éirinn, the king is married to the very land, both spiritually and physically. There was a time when the High King of Teamhair was guided by wise and astute counsellors, constantly reminding him of his obligation to his people and the earth beneath his feet. That was then, but this is now. The King was being controlled, and he had capitulated on his responsibilities and his sacred oath. Rogues and opportunists saw the king's weaknesses, plying him senseless with physical pleasures. Mead and wine flowed like fresh spring water keeping Fionntan weak and amused. It was said that depending how drunk the king was, his subjects were only too pleased to share his generosity. The king had apparently become the court fool.

Francach was a boastful man, and it was well known that he had Fomorian blood running through his cold veins. He was large and aggressive, and it was said that he carried a sword so deadly, that it must possess an angry, blood thirsty spirit. As the kings champion he had the king's ear, and it could be said that in recent times, it was Francach the warrior who really held sway over Éirinn. Unfortunately for Éirinn, Francach was a man of no principles and dark intentions, and not being a Gael didn't give a silver coin for the land or its people. Francach's heart was as black as the clothes on his back. The people who served the king, if that's the right word, were terrified of Francach for he was a man without friends, who trusted no one, and stories say, that anyone who crossed him never saw the next light of day, well, that's what we in the village heard.

Don't misunderstand what I'm saying about the man. He wasn't just a brute, for he was as crafty as a feral cat and his cunning had become well known to the lesser kings of the other four provinces. One or two of them had tried to plead with Fionntan that Francach was a dangerous man and should be given a wide berth, but unfortunately Fionntan was growing weaker by the day under the influence of his champion and his evil, mischievous spirit. It wasn't long before one of the lesser kings had an unfortunate accident, and the finger of suspicion pointed right back towards Teamhair and the man in black, although none could prove he was involved. The fear that was generated prevented a direct confrontation, no one wished to fall victim to a man who dabbled in the black arts, so not a word was uttered against him, well at least not out loud. In the meantime, Francach grew more powerful as the old king continued to weaken his own authority.

It was about this time that the land showed signs of sickness. Animals began to die from strange illnesses, crops withered and died on the stem and no fruit appeared on the trees. The winters became unusually extreme, the cold wind was bitter, the snows were blinding and the rains were unceasing. Even humans were not immune to the change as no babies were conceived or born. Éirinn was sick and she was dying.

Lulach the bard strummed the strings of his harp and remembered the days when all was well within the walls of Teamhair. He sat in the corner of the main hall with his back to the window and the ills of the outside world, concluding that the ills on the outside of Teamhair were a direct consequence of the badness practiced within. He was a good and discerning Bard and a diligent harpist having been taught by a Druid of the Silver

Branch. Besides his mastery of the harp, Lulach was fairly competent in the Draoi, which is the Druid skills, and he saw with his own eyes the corruption at the high seat of Éirinn. Until recently, Lulach had felt reasonably safe here at Teamhair, but things were changing and changing fast. It appeared that the spirit that resided within the very being of Francach had concluded that Lulach was a danger to its existence, and that he must be disposed of sooner than later. Francach was alerted in a dream, waking in the middle of the night with beads of sweat glistening on his brow.

"The bard, the damned bard," he shouted. "Get the bard, he's a traitor and he's scheming to kill the king," he screamed at the guard as he flung his bedchamber door open.

"Go on man, arrest the bard, kill him if you wish, I don't care, just get him."

The guard looked totally confused, but after a moment of hesitation ran off down the corridor to apprehend Lulach the bard.

Francach reached for his sword, "kill him Francach, kill the bard," squealed the spirit. Francach raced out of the bedchamber with his sword waving in his hand. As Francach approached the room of Lulach, the door was already open. The guard stood there looking around, but Lulach was gone. In the middle of the room was a bowl of water and a candle on a nearby stand.

Francach drew closer, "what magic is this?" he hissed, as he brought his sword down hard on the bowl, smashing it into a thousand pieces.

"Divination my lord," stuttered the guard, "I've heard tell the Druids can see the future using only a bowl of water and a candle."

Francach flung his arms high in the air, his face red and contorted with anger and screamed, "Horse shit, you let him go you incompetent dog."

The guard backed off, only to fall backwards over Lulach's music stool and just as well he did, for at that moment the sword of Francach came thundering down smashing everything in its arc. Quickly, and with a great deal of panic, the guard scurried out into the corridor and running for his dear life made as much room between Francach and himself as possible.

In the meantime, Francach continued to bellow obscenities and rain blows on anything or anyone that stood between him and the young bard. Fortunately, Lulach was well gone.

Corn dollies and Sun wheels

The day had broken for over an hour when Sorcha and I entered the smithy. "Sorry we're late Eóghann," I called apologetically.

Silence! Not a sound.

"Eóghann, are you there?"

"He's gone, his things are gone," cried Sorcha, with real disappointment in her voice.

Not wanting to dampen Sorcha's enthusiasm I suggested that we should start making the Corn dollies and Sun wheels without him. Sorcha seemed okay with that, so we sat in the hay and started to make the images. After about an hour and what seemed like a dozen attempts to construct the first dolly, Sorcha and I decided to take a break.

"Finished already?" came a soft voice from right behind us. It was Eóghann.

"Okay, that's pretty good," said Eóghann politely. "Everything you make contains your own intentions," he said.

"Eóghann, what are we making these things for?" I enquired, with a touch of frustration in my voice.

"Orla, Corn Dollies are a representation of the fruit of the Great Mother. When we offer a Corn Dolly to her, we are showing our gratitude for what she has supplied. She sustains us through the years turning, and we offer our thanks in return. The Sun Wheel is symbolic of the Universal Fathers ride through the year. He is the bringer of warmth and light, he is the father of all that lives upon the Mother. It is his love that fertilises Mother Earth so that the life they both love is sustained in all things." "Orla, can you think of anything more important to make at this time?"

"I cannot think of any reason why making stupid Corn Dollies and Sun Wheels is going to help saving the people of Éirinn," countered Orla churlishly.

"Orla, do you trust me?"

"I trust you," chirped Sorcha.

Orla cast her sister a dismissive look and turned away. "I hate this rain, I'm tired, damp and utterly miserable," muttered Orla sitting down in the hay.

Eóghann paced up and down, ignoring Orla's mood. He took up some straw, sat down, and preceded to begin the making of another Corn Dolly.

The two girls sat and watched as Eóghann made several Corn Dollies and Sun Wheels, they also noticed that none of them were complete.

"Why are you not finishing what you are making?" enquired Orla, now a little less petulant.

Eóghann looked up with those strange ancient eyes and said, "I cannot do this alone, you have to help me."

Orla slowly reached down and lifted the first Corn Dolly and began to complete it. Her sister watching very closely followed her example and began to copy her.

There was a long silence in the barn as the three of them industriously completed their task.

"Enough," cried Eóghann, "We're finished."

"How many have we made," asked Sorcha?

"Twenty-seven of each"

"That's a funny number, why twenty-seven?" retorted Sorcha.

Orla stood up holding her back, and by the tone of her voice, it was obvious that she didn't grasp the meaning of the number. "Twenty-seven, who cares whether it's twenty-seven, or seventy-seven my backs aching and I'm hungry. I'm going back to the house, Sorcha, come."

Before Sorcha could rise, Eóghann reached into his bag and pulled out a loaf of bread and a whole cooked chicken.

Both girls stopped dead and stared at the food before them.

Eóghann continued to dip into his bag, and this time he lifted out 3 of the rosiest apples you have ever seen. Next appeared a bunch of what looked like small cherries, except they were green. A water skin was next, but it wasn't water that came out, it was golden and sweet and the smell was wonderful and overpowering.

"There's enough here for everyone, if you'd like to stay." Smiled Eóghann.

Sorcha's eyes were popping out of her head, "Oh, yes please, Orla, Orla, wait, can we stay, can we?"

"Okay, we'll stay, but only if you tell us what's so special about twenty-seven." Orla said through salivating lips.

The three sat down and Eóghann divided the food between five.

After a moment, and in between mouthfuls of delicious food Eóghann began to explain about the number twenty-seven.

"There are twenty-seven standing stones surrounding Teamhair, supplying the great mound with a constant flow of Earth energy. In return, the mound spreads energy outwards across the land ... blessing it. The fulcrum of this energy is the high king. He is the key between the Gaels, Great Goddess Mother Earth and the Danann deities. When all these things are in harmony, Éirinn will prosper and her people will grow fat with plenty. Yet, if the king should turn away, or be turned away from the ancient ways ... Éirinn and her people will suffer. I have come from Brugh Na Bóinne and the house of my father to right a wrong and to save Éirinn from destruction, will you help me Orla?"

"Where's Brugh na Bóinne Orla?" chirped Sorcha, "where is it, is it far?"

"I don't know Sorcha," replied Orla, looking at Eóghann for an answer.

"I'll tell you all you want to know later", said Eóghann, "Each standing stone must have a Corn Dolly and a Sun Wheel attached ... will you help me complete this work?"

Orla stood up and her head was spinning, "How do I know what you say is true, why, we only met yesterday, you could be a thief and a liar" although she really knew that that was not so.

The food and the depth of conversation was just too much for little Sorcha, she leaned back against a soft sack of animal feed and promptly fell asleep.

"I was hoping she would do that", smiled Eóghann, "Small children never keep secrets ... never have done".

Eóghann continued, "To the East of Teamhair, the stone that greets the rising sun has the imprint of a hand, a small hand, a girl's hand. On the morning of the Summer Solstice when all preparations have been completed, the girl must place her hand into the imprint on the stone for the energies to be restored."

"You think that I am this girl, don't you," said Orla, in a disbelieving tone?

Eóghann walked around as if searching for the right words, and then for what seemed like an eternity he spoke, "Orla, a few days ago you were invited by Cathal the Druid to speak at the Village Elders meeting, do you remember? Before she had time to respond Eóghann continued, "You were the only person there that believed that Danu the Great Goddess of the Flowing Waters would intervene; is that not so?"

He continued, "That night, you were wrapped up against the cold as you made your way to the smithy, and there you saw a Vixen, correct?"

"Yes, but!" Orla stuttered, completely out of her depth.

"The Goddess moves around her people although not always easily recognisable", Eóghann said quietly. "Teamhair is in ruin, and dark clouds lie over her. Negative forces have taken hold and the vengeance of the Fomorians is moving to fulfilment."

"Eóghann, what has that to do with the Vixen I saw?" cried Orla.

"The Vixen you saw was Danu, Orla; she listened to your heart and the words that came from your mouth. Your destiny was written from the beginning of time; Danu came to affirm the truth of her daughter."

Eóghann moved to the door, observing the black rolling clouds and the steady rain, then quickly turning he said, "Tonight we will prepare to go to Teamhair, we will leave in the morning ... and Orla, don't tell anyone, okay?"

Lulach, Bard of Teamhair

The one thing about Lulach, he was a born survivor, and having experienced the black temper of Francach first hand, there was no way he was going to hang around Teamhair. Hang being the operative word here. He had witnessed Francach's cruelty only recently, having seen many a good soul dispatched to the Summerlands for nothing more than being in the wrong place at the wrong time, and this was no time to try to reason with someone who was as bad tempered as a hog with a headache.

Across the open fields the summer wind blew rain like arrows, and Lulach pulled his bardic robe closer to his body. His first thoughts were escape and survival and so as soon as he passed through the main gates he more or less went in the direction his legs took him, which in all fairness, was a straight line down the main road leading to and from Teamhair.

The open air and driving rain began to clear his thoughts and he reasoned that if he was pursued, Francach's men would soon find him, therefore, he took to the open fields. The truth was, back in Teamhair Francach had calmed down and personally couldn't give a fiddlers bowstring about the stupid bard. Lulach unfortunately didn't know that and continued at a pace with the intention of putting as much distance between Francach and himself as possible.

The clouds thinned out enough for our young bard to get a reasonable glimpse of the watery sun, and collecting his thoughts, calculated the direction of the druid island. Keeping the main road in view, and considering the difficult conditions, he kept up quite a pace and after a few hours he concluded that it was safe to take a rest.

Finding a grove of trees he looked around for some that had grown up in close proximity, knowing that the branches would be intertwined and probably a good shelter from the rain. Soon he found what he was looking for, a group of mighty oaks growing together as tight as a shrunken shoe. Here he found a reasonably dry spot on which to sit and eat the piece of hard bread that he always had in his pocket. Let me explain, Lulach was a popular chap around Teamhair, and sometimes he would sing or tell stories to the kitchen staff ... his reward would be a little extra something to eat. Anyway, not meaning to digress, Lulach sat down and ate his bread and before long, he was asleep.

"Well, you are a pretty sight, master Bard", came a voice close by.

Lulach woke with a start, banging his head in the process.

"Who's there?" called Lulach, expecting the worst and rubbing his head.

Then stepping from the nearby bushes appeared an elderly man. He was dressed in the Raven feather robes of a Druid of the Silver Branch. Lulach sat back in amazement. "Lord Druid, why are you here, so far of the road?"

"I could ask you the same question master Bard, but that would be wasting time," spoke the Druid, keeping his hood over his head

"Time, time for what?" stuttered the Bard. Then, as if remembering his place, began to apologise for asking such an impertinent question.

The Druid slowly walked over to the tree opposite and sat down.

"Lulach, tell me about Teamhair ... I want to know everything?" asked the mystery Druid.

Lulach was now in a state of shock, not to mention being half out of his wits.

The Druid opposite raised his hand and drew back his hood.

"Master Cathal" said Lulach in amazement and relief, "I haven't seen or heard from you in many a long year, what brings you here so close to Teamhair?"

"I'll answer all your questions soon master Bard, first tell me everything about what is going on in Teamhair?"

Lulach went on to relate all that had been happening over the last couple of seasons, and how the King's champion had caste some kind of spell over King Fionntan, finishing with his own experience with Francach and his escape.

The old Druid sat and pondered, staying silent for some considerable time.

Suddenly, the Druid spoke, "Lulach, I have to go to Teamhair ... I have to speak with the High King. The Druid High Council has instructed me to talk to the King and bring him back to his senses. Yet, what you have told me; it appears that the High King is not in control at Teamhair, and that Teamhair is in the hands of a Fomorian. The situation is indeed dangerous and this would account why Éirinn is sick. Lulach, I must leave you here for an hour or two, I promise you I will be back before the sun touches the tops of those trees over there. If on the other hand I do not return by then, assume that something is wrong and make your way to the Druids Island and inform the High Council of what you know".

At that Cathal got to his feet, embraced the Bard and left.

Lulach looked around the grove and satisfied that he was alone closed his eyes and began to hum a Bardic chant that takes him into another dimension. Within a few minutes he could feel his consciousness of this place being replaced by something else. The tall trees were replaced by glistening stone blocks, the sound of the wind through the trees was replaced by singing, and the smells of the forest were replaced by the sweet scent of other-worldly fragrances. The Bard could also hear voices, then, as if a curtain had been raised people came into vision. Stood before him were four tall beautiful people who bowed and greeted him, offering him food and drink. Lulach accepted these things graciously. He looked enquiringly into the drinking vessel and saw what could only be described as liquid gold, the smell was sweet and wonderful and the taste was like no other. The food, which he had placed in his lap, was like no other food he had seen. There was a stalk with lots of little branches, and on these little branches were a kind of fruit. The fruit was green yet as sweet as honey, such fruit he had never had. There was also bread and cheese of a taste and texture foreign to him. The tastes and smells intoxicated him until his head swam.

"Am I dead?" he said in a low voice.

"No Lulach, you are not dead," said one of the tall people, "You are in the Halls of your Deities, tell us what you want, perhaps we may give it to you?"

Lulach looking at each person in turn said, "You have an advantage over me, you know who I am, yet I have no knowledge of you. You could be Francach's evil spirit trying to deceive me ... identify yourselves and I may tell you my business."

One of the four stepped forward and began to recite Lulach's family tree, within a few seconds all of Lulach's ancestors had been named as far back as the invasion.

It was common knowledge that part of the Druidic learning process was to set to memory their own family line as an exercise, and frighteningly, this person knew Lulach's line as if it were his own.

"You have to be one of my ancestors to have that kind of knowledge," snapped Lulach.

"Not quite young Bard, we know your ancestors, if fact, they are never far away from you ... as are we," smiled the person who stood opposite.

"I came to seek council from my guides," said Lulach. "I am only a Bard; I don't know what to do. This thing ... this, this problem is far too big for the likes of me, that is why I hummed the 'Other World' chant, so that perhaps the answers would be forthcoming. I never expected to meet ... you, whoever you are."

"Young Bard, we are the Sons and Daughters of the Goddess

Danu, and what is happening in Teamhair is known to us," explained the tall figure. "We will tell you what you must do and after we have given you your instructions, you must turn around and return to Teamhair."

By now Lulach was shaking in fear and awe at the figures before him as the four Danann's gave him his instructions.

"Lulach, Lulach, in the name of all the Gods do you always sleep when there is so much to do?" barked a familiar voice.

"Cathal, it's you?" responded Lulach, "you'll never guess where I've been?"

Cathal grabbed him by the scruff of his cloak and retorted angrily, "You think this is a time for guessing games? This is a time for action, a time for putting right a terrible wrong. Éirinn is dying and all you can think about is 'guessing games', grab your things we must be off."

"No Cathal wait, that's not what I meant."

Cathal released his tight grip on the Bard, who proceeded to fall backwards, rather undignified on to his bottom.

"Well?" Bellowed Cathal; waiting for an answer.

Lulach rose to his feet rather slowly and sheepishly, and rubbing his rear end continued to explain all that had happened while the Druid had been away.

The old Druid frowned, and looking the Bard directly in the eye, spoke, "Lulach, do you believe that what you saw and heard is true?"

"Yes, I do," said the young Bard.

Just then a vixen stepped out of the bushes nearby and faced them. Both men spun around. Lulach being the younger of the two was the first to react, reaching down for his staff.

"No, that won't be necessary, we are in no danger," whispered Cathal, holding the young Bards arm.

Cathal the Druid raising his arms, made a Sigel in the air, saying with great reverence, "Lady Danu, I understand."

Immediately the vixen bowed her head to the ground and disappeared as quickly as she came.

"You can close your mouth now Lulach, and yes, I have great hopes for you young man, tomorrow is a big day for all of us, mark my words," said Cathal in a surprisingly optimistic tone.

A Guest in Teamhair

Fionntan, the High King of Éirinn sat slumped in his chair. The usual business of court passed him by as if he was but a mere spectator. Out of bleary eyes, he could see the familiar faces, yet focusing and maintaining eye contact with any individual was impossible but voices he could hear. Sometimes he could put faces to voices in his mind, but he found it hard to respond when somebody spoke directly to him. Most in the court considered Fionntan to be drunk, or even mad, even his closest advisors began to think that it was high time that Fionntan was replaced as High King. How people soon forget. Fionntan the wise he used to be called, Fionntan the great is what many in court said about him, yet now, only derision and kitchen jokes.

Across the court staring at the King was Francach the black, scheming and strengthening his grip over Teamhair. Raising his drinking cup to his mouth to disguise his smirk, he was confident that nobody knew his secret. Watching the High Kings head bobbing this way and that in an apparent drunken stupor, he imagined the ultimate satisfaction of watching the complete collapse of the Gaels in Éirinn.

"Not long now" he thought, as he sensed the total indifference of the regional Kings … "You will die with your beloved Éirinn, idiots, all of you."

The guard stood at the main outer gate, cold and miserable. The rain, although a little lighter, was still falling.

"I'd rather be stood up to my neck in horse shit than be here on this horrible day," he muttered to himself.

He pulled his hood and cloak a little higher in an attempt to keep out the damp. Looking up at the wall he saw a colleague.

"Any chance of a warm drink down here," he called optimistically.

Sadly his colleague had moved on.

"By all that is sacred, a man could die down here without being missed," he grumbled to himself.

Just then, he got the fright of his life as someone tapped him on the shoulder. He was so startled by the unexpected event he almost wet himself. Turning quickly, he anticipated the worst as the color drained from his face.

"No need to be so jumpy young man, I don't think your intimidated by an old woman, are you? A big strapping warrior like yourself."

Standing before him was a little old woman wrapped in a colourless rough woollen shawl. In her hand was a wooden bowl of steaming thick broth, which she offered him with a slight bow.

Recovering his embarrassment, he coughed giving himself time to gather his senses.

"Er, that's very kind of you to take pity on a poor soldier like myself," he coughed again.

He took the broth and raised the bowl to his lips, oh, how good that tasted as he let the warm delicious liquid flow slowly down the back of his throat. He closed his eyes, and for a moment he thought he could hear his own beloved mother's voice talking to him. The broth reminded him of home. He opened his eyes and smacked his lips noticing that the cold had disappeared from his body and his mind was filled with wonderful thoughts of Ulster.

He looked down to where the old woman had been standing but she was gone. The only reminder that she was ever there was the wooden bowl in his hand and a tuft of reddish animal hair on the ground where she had been stood.

Turning to the gate he looked to see if she had slipped by him, but there was no one to be seen, just a few horse tracks in the mud, including, seemingly those of a dog.

The guard pulled his hood up over his head again and went

about his business whistling a tune that he remembered from his boyhood. "Happy days," he thought, "Happy days."

In the halls of the King, Francach was meeting with his counsellors and informing them of his wishes for the upcoming celebration of the Summer Solstice. It was his duty, or so he said, to stand in for the King as the King is unfortunately too ill to officiate. Therefore, all tributes will be given to him in the Kings absence. The counsellors salivated at the thought of all that wealth that would soon be resting in their greedy, sweaty hands, for once the tributes had been paid, the King was surplus to requirements and could be disposed off. In the meantime, he could sit on his throne and babble like a baby for all to see, a necessity if the plan was to be a success.

At the back of the hall stood a small shadowy figure, watching and listening to all that was going on. The rough woolly cloak pulled up so nobody would see the tears in the otherworldly eyes of the woman whose heart reached out to Fionntan High King of Éirinn, and to the land itself.

The King although not conscious of the presence of the person watching him, could feel the impact of being observed.

He moved uncomfortably, shifting this way and that, his head turning in all directions, his eyes blinking, trying to focus in the direction of the unseen energy probing his very soul.

Francach, ever watchful and vigilant couldn't help but see the King's unusual behaviour, jumped to his feet and turning slowly, eyes ever watchful, signalled his guards to close the doors. Once the doors were closed, Francach began to search the room with his eyes for any strangers or persons present who were acting in a strange manner. He was no fool, in fact, he didn't get where he was, by walking this world with his eyes closed.

"Where are you?" he whispered to himself, "I know you're in this room somewhere, whoever you are."

It was no easy task spotting someone in a crowded room full of moving people, but Francach was a wily character, full of deceit, and he was an old hand at this particular game. His eyes flirted this way and that, looking and probing all areas of the room.

"Damn these stupid Gaels, why can't they ever stand still?" he murmured.

Then he saw something, a small figure in a cloak, placed in the shadow between two large windows, one of which was slightly open. In the shadow he couldn't see the person, but he could make out that the person was paying too much attention to Fionntan. Without causing any interest in himself, he slowly and quietly moved from his table. Moving through the crowded hall in the opposite direction, he moved through the people in a wide arc, staying close to the wall and never taking his eyes off the person in the cloak.

"I've got you now," he thought, as he pulled a scian dubh from his belt.

He was now only a few paces behind the person in the cloak, and he moved with the grace of a skilled warrior. Patiently waiting his opportunity, a gap opened in the crowd and he moved with speed and precision. The knife went through the cloak like butter, and the cloak collapsed to the floor empty of any person or entity that had been within it.

Francach, shocked and confused let go of the knife, stepping back in bewilderment.

"What kind of trickery is this?" he bellowed, startling all around him, and in total frustration he kicked the cloak and anyone else who was near enough for him to reach.

His face reddened with rage. "Guards, guards," he shrieked. "Block all the exits," And lifting the cloak up of the floor, yelled, "I want the owner of this cloak here, in this room, I'm going to slit his throat whoever it is." "Bring him here now, right now."

The crowd by now had wisely taken several steps backwards,

leaving Francach to demolish a couple of tables and chairs as his fury raged.

After a few minutes, his temper began to subside and he grimaced at the crowd and made his way back to his chair, the crowd opened up like a new furrowed field to let him through. In his hand was the Cloak of rough wool, which he threw unceremoniously on the table in front of him. He snatched a cup of mead from a trembling servant nearby, and drank it down in one gulp; the servant dutifully topped it up again, in fact, several times. Eventually, Francach's head dropped forward, his eyes closed and he began to snore like an old hog. He may have been a formidable warrior, but he was no drinker. The people around about him looking relieved made for the door … but the door and all of the other exits were closed.

Well, as you can imagine the party was over, and Francach was the party pooper. Everybody would just have to wait until he woke and then, perhaps they would be allowed to leave.

The rough woollen cloak lay on the table, just where it had been thrown, and all that could be seen on it was a few reddish animal hairs and a small hole where the knife had gone through it.

Francach began to stir, and smacking his lips and opening his eyes he looked around.

People close by started to stare and other heads turned as they became aware he had woken.

"Stop looking at me," he croaked, kicking over another chair. "Where's my prisoner?"

He jumped to his feet. People scattered in all directions at his sudden movement.

A servant passed within reach, and Francach grabbed him by the scruff of his shirt, "Fetch me some water you useless oaf." The servant on being released ran off in the direction of the kitchen.

"Well" called out Francach, "Where's my bloody prisoner?"

The captain of the guard moved nervously closer.

"Well?" growled Francach, "Where's my prisoner?"

"Er! It appears that the person, whoever it is, has the ability to pass through walls, my lord."

Francach looked him in the eye, and raising his arms gesturing in expectation for more, repeated, "Yes, you imbecile, and ... where is my prisoner?"

"Gone my lord, I'm afraid the owner of that cloak," pointing with his finger, "Is gone."

Francach was coming to the boil again.

It was unfortunate that the servant came back with water at this time, because no sooner had he placed it on the table, Francach punched him, knocking him over a table. With only his pride seriously hurt and maybe a loose tooth, the servant scrambled to his feet holding his face, made for the relative safety of the far side of the room.

The captain of the guard was now backing away in fear of Francach's temper.

"Don't you move away from me when I'm talking to you." Francach hissed.

As if frozen, the captain was still pointing at the cloak, and as quick as a flash the scian dubh arched through the air removing the end of the captain's finger.

The captain howled in shock and pain and fell to his knees. Francach towered over him, "I will not tolerate failure, next time it will be your head I will remove, do you understand me?"

"Yes my lord," whimpered the captain.

"Open the doors captain ... this day is over."

"Yes my lord, sorry my lord." The captain rose up holding his bleeding hand.

Just then Francach moved closer, as if embracing his captain. The captain's legs buckled and he fell backwards, hitting a chair on the way down.

Francach stood holding a bloody knife in his hand. "Sorry he

said, I don't do sorry, anyway, I need a captain with ten fingers."
"Take him out and bury him, and clean this mess up."

Picking up the woollen cloak off the table, Francach sneered down at it, then in the language of the ancient Fomorians he spat to himself in an undertone, "Peasants, useless bloody peasants," as he tossed the cloak at a guard. "Burn it."

The Story Unfolds

"Where are we?" Orla asked.

"Just beneath the hill of Teamhair," said Eóghann, as he gathered up a little bundle of dead wood and kindling.

"Eóghann, what are we doing here?" Orla shivered, as it was a little chilly under the tree canapé.

"Let me start the fire and I'll explain everything,"

Orla sat back against a tree, and it was as if the tree sighed against her back. The breeze was light in the woods, and the suns watery rays cutting through the rain clouds were changed from summer gold to a beautiful shade of green. The smell of damp wood and woodland flowers was intoxicating, and very soon Orla's eyes had closed and she soon drifted into sleep.

Orla woke to Eóghann's voice, "Orla, Orla, take this it will warm you." In Eóghann's outstretched arm was a bowl of hot steaming broth.

"How long have I been asleep," Orla yawned, taking the bowl.

"A little while, feeling better now?"

She then noticed that a rough woollen cloak had been carefully wrapped around her to keep out the chill.

"Eóghann, this cloak … whose is it?" She took another sip of the broth.

She was met by a wry smile as he took his bowl and sat against the tree opposite.

Eóghann finished his broth and closing his eyes and to all intents and purposes, he appeared to be sleeping.

Orla looked around at the nearby trees and bushes, wondering why she trusted this young man so much. Maybe it was the atmosphere, maybe she was just growing up, after all, she was almost a woman now, but she felt happy, happier than she had felt in a long time. It was then that her thoughts drifted to her village, and her parents. Boy, were they going to be mad at her unexpected disappearance. She began to worry, and to imagine that they would believe that Eóghann had kidnapped her, and of all the awful things that could befall a young girl at the hands of an unscrupulous Reiver.

"I've got to go back, I can't stay here," she mumbled to herself.

She looked nervously across at Eóghann but he hadn't moved.

She leaned forward from the tree as she prepared to rise to her feet and make her escape, and then she heard a noise to her left and sat back quickly at hearing the sound.

Eóghann hadn't moved a muscle.

She waited a few moments and listened. Silence! She leaned forward again, keeping her eyes on Eóghann.

Crunch! She jumped at the sudden sound, and by now she had started to perspire with the tension and she needed to shed the woollen cloak. Again, she moved her head very slowly to where she thought the sound had come from. Then she saw it, a Vixen, standing about fifteen strides away, and looking her in the eye.

Orla gasped and looked over at Eóghann, he was still leaning against the tree ... but his eyes were open looking back at her.

"Eóghann, a fox," she whispered, breathing heavy.

"A vixen, if you don't mind," came a voice from her left.

Orla swung her head round and saw a brightly shining woman standing in exactly the same spot the Vixen had been standing.

Eóghann suddenly sprang to his feet and bowed, "Welcome lady Danu, I have been expecting you."

Orla gasped, wrestled herself out of the cloak and on her knees, bowing her head before the Great Mother, and with much trembling began to mutter some prayer she had learned from Cathal many years before.

Eóghann walked across the patch and raised Orla to her feet, but her legs gave way and she fell back onto her knees.

It was obvious that Orla was as unprepared as any mortal at meeting the Great Goddess, and with her eyes firmly shut tight and repeating Cathal's prayer, she had blanked out everything around her.

After several long minutes, Orla still crouching close to the ground peeped fearfully through half closed fingers.

"Perhaps I should have appeared to you as a donkey," responded Danu, "Maybe you wouldn't have been so startled."

"Come along my dear, stand up and let me see you," said Danu, rather mischievously. "Anyone would think I had all day. Well, I really have got all day, in fact I've got all day every day, being an immortal."

"Stand up, stand up, the time for you and your kind is almost imminent".

Orla rose to her feet supported by Eóghann.

Danu opened her arms and something wondrous and magical happened. Within the open space of her arms around ball appeared, cloudy at first, and then began to clear. In the ball Orla could see people gathered, a man in black appeared to be giving orders, and the High King himself was there sitting, dozing in his chair.

"Mother, what is this, and what is happening?" cried Orla.

"Watch and see," replied Danu.

The magical ball showed all that had happened in the Hall of the High King of Teamhair from just before the rains began to fall. It showed how Francach the Fomorian had craftily infiltrated Teamhair and wove his evil web over the land. Orla watched in absolute astonishment as the incident with Lulach, the Bard of Teamhair, unfolded within the orb, and how Lulach had luckily escaped the clutches of Francach. Next she was shown the conversations within the Druid sanctuary and how Cathal had been instructed to investigate Éirinn's demise. She even saw the dream that Lulach had with the Danann's.

There was a long lull before Orla spoke and then she nervously and quietly whispered.

"What has this to do with me as I am of little importance in this land? My father is a humble blacksmith of common stock, and my mother likewise."

Danu seemed to grow in stature and raised her hands, forcing Orla to step back in awe.

"Orla, you are the daughter of Branan and Gràinne, you are also the daughter of every man and woman in Éirinn and you are the embodiment of every daughter and every son on this beautiful green emerald isle.

I stand before you and ask, yes ask, if you will follow my instructions and free Éirinn of this malady. Orla, golden one, will you do what I ask of you?"

Orla was by now trembling with the unexpected, and tears were running freely down her cheeks.

"Mother, tell me what it is that I must do … and I will willingly do it."

Danu sank back to what appeared to be a normal size, and Orla breathed a little more easily.

Eóghann gave her some warm broth and wrapped her in the rough woollen cloak that had lain at her feet, and seated her against the tree. She sipped at the broth and pulled the cloak a little tighter around her neck, she shivered.

"Eóghann, the cloak, its turning blue," she called out in surprise.

"Yes, I'll explain that later, if that's alright," he answered reassuringly with a smile.

Danu stood in the centre of the clearing and never moved a muscle, in fact, Orla thought she resembled a statue and started to question her own mind as to whether this was just a strange dream she was having.

"You're not dreaming."

"What?" jumped Orla, surprised?

"I said you're not dreaming," came a soft voice from Danu, "We are waiting for the others to arrive and then we can begin."

"Others?" Orla looked towards Eóghann for an answer but none was coming.

Suddenly, voices could be heard through the trees and Orla felt a sudden rush of panic. She looked across the clearing towards Danu who held out her hand, inviting Orla to step closer to her. Orla moved towards Danu and took her hand in hers. Instantly, her fears subsided and it reminded her of her own mother's warm touch. She stood by the Goddess and watched in the direction of the voices ... suddenly old Cathal appeared with a younger man following in his footsteps.

Cathal's face was a picture of surprise.

"Orla, what are you doing here so far from home," spluttered the old Druid, "And who are these people ... tell me child?"

Before Orla could speak Danu released Orla's hand and transformed herself into a vixen. Moving towards the Druids she regained her form and spoke.

"Cathal my old friend, it's been a long time since you first saw me mapping out your future."

The old Druid sank to his knees, and with head bowed he began to speak.

"Lady Danu, thank the Gods that you are here and that you are aware of Éirinn's plight."

Standing directly behind the kneeling Cathal, Lulach stood ridged and as white as a linen sheet.

"Please close your mouth young man or I will change into something more awe inspiring and give you a good reason to stand with your mouth open before your Goddess."

Immediately Lulach closed his mouth and fell to his knees behind Cathal burying his head in the old Druids cloak.

After several minutes and much coaxing from Orla both men rose to their feet, Lulach's legs appeared to be independent from his brain and it took a few moments for him to look anywhere near normal again.

"Lady," Cathal addressed the Goddess. "Please excuse my young friend as this is the first time he has stood before the mother of all."

"Stood, you say Cathal," the Goddess said in an undertone.

Orla couldn't help but smile at the humour in Danu's choice of words.

"Eat and rest, for in a little while the appointed time will be upon us," Danu held her arms open towards Eóghann who had before him food to sustain four persons. "The other's who are due to arrive have already eaten, and they will be ready and prepared for the task ahead."

With that said, and in the blink of an eye, she was gone.

Cathal, Lulach and Orla looked enquiringly at each other and then towards Eóghann.

"Who is coming?" asked Lulach.

"You can ask them yourself, young Bard," smiled Eóghann, "They're here."

At the edge of the clearing stood an army of tall, graceful men and woman, each carrying weapons of precious materials and studded with what appeared to be pulsing glistening stones.

"These are my people," declared Eóghann, "The people of the Goddess Danu ... Our mother ... And your mother. Today Éirinn will be made whole again."

Summer Solstice

The sun was climbing in the sky and the appointed time for Éirinn's restoration was almost here. Orla, still looking somewhat overawed by all that was happening around her cleared her mind by closing her eyes and thinking of life back in the village. It seemed so far away.

The Danann's had settled down in and around the clearing, and had fallen into groups chatting amongst themselves. Eóghann passed between each group nodding his understanding and approval at what was explained to him. It seemed that a plan had been orchestrated.

"Lulach," Whispered Cathal, "Find out what's happening I don't like the idea of being left out in the dark."

"Master Cathal, these people are speaking a different language to us, how am I supposed to understand what they are saying?" returned the young Bard.

Lulach realised that he had perhaps spoken a little too loudly because the whole area had fallen silent, and all eyes were upon him and Cathal.

Stepping from the trees, a young woman stepped forward and walked towards the two Druids. She was dressed all in silver and she reflected the sheen of the forest. With each step she appeared to change colour … light green, dark green, gold and yellow, brown and red. The Druids were stunned at her figure and stepped back as she approached them.

"Have no fear Master Druids," she spoke in the tongue of the Gael. "I have come to explain to you what you wanted to know." She smiled a comforting smile and then explained the plan that the Goddess had formulated.

As the young Danann woman was finishing answering the Druids questions a small light began to emerge at the far side of the clearing. Some of the Danann groups nearest to the light began to spread out in expectation of what was happening, and as they retreated the light began to expand. Within a few moments the light had grown to the size of a large disc about the height of a tall man. The light seemed to pulse like that of a star on the darkest night, so bright that those close by had to shield their eyes. Then suddenly, out of the centre of the pulsing disk stepped the Goddess Danu along with Ceana, Druidess and leader of the High Druid Council followed by Oisian, Coinneach and Brighde. Ceana and the three Druids of the high council spun round in total confusion.

"What is this place and how did we get here?" spluttered Ceana, looking at the others.

Cathal pushed forward and standing before the four Druids made a sweeping bow.

"Ceana and fellow Druids, allow me to introduce you to our guests and perhaps settle your minds as to why we have been gathered here."

Suddenly aware of his presumptuous action, Cathal quickly turned towards the Goddess for her permission.

"You appear to be capable and prepared for what is required, perhaps you would like to explain what is happening and what is about to happen next." The Goddess said in an almost humorous tone.

"Lady Danu, please forgive me for overstepping my authority," Cathal whispered with a bow of his head.

"Yes, yes, let's get on with it," snapped Danu, "You Gaels are so unpredictable ... perhaps that's why I love you so much."

At that she looked over at Orla, smiled and graciously nodded.

As the Druids huddled together discussing what was happening, Orla walked over to Eóghann who had entered into dialogue with a group of Danann's.

"Orla, you look fine in blue," quipped Eóghann, for by now the rough woollen cloak had turned the most fabulous blue you could imagine. There were nods of approval from the gathered warriors.

The Danann's appeared to be highly organised, unlike the Druids who were still picking through the bones of everything that they had been told, although eventually they would sort themselves out, they always did, it just takes time.

Orla's eyes were darting everywhere, from the beautiful Danann warriors across to the gesturing Druids. The Goddess had expanded again; at least that is how she appeared to Orla, she thought she was at least a full head and shoulders above everyone else there present. The one thing she was sure of though, was Danu had returned to statue mode, not a movement or a blink of the eyes, nothing … not a twitch. It was like she had left her body standing there, if body is the right word, and wandered off somewhere in spirit form.

Whatever spirit resided within Francach it was becoming aware that something was going on and was becoming more and more agitated. The big powerful brute that was Francach was looking nervous and unkempt, his eyes were red through lack of real sleep, and his skin had changed from the usual healthy pink to a strange dusty grey colour. Some of his soldiers thought he was dead and that some evil entity was still residing within him, in a way they were right. Francach sat slouched in a chair directly opposite the King, staring, glaring and muttering under his breath. By this time any people in the great hall had made rather a large distance between the seething Fomorian and themselves, a kind of safety zone because by now Francach's outbursts had become more often and increasingly more violent.

Servants began to cry off sick and were sometimes dragged into service by Francach's guard, even the guards themselves were not immune to the black lords' evil temper, and even they kept a healthy distance between him and themselves.

"I should kill him now and done with it," Francach hissed to himself.

"No, not yet, we've invested too much into this plan to throw it away at the eleventh hour ... sit back, relax and be patient."

Out on the walls of Teamhair the guards were occupying every available niche and doorway to escape becoming soaked through to the skin, and although they were well trained and alert regardless of the adverse conditions, none of them was aware of the spirit that moved within their midst. One by one the guards sank gently to the floor locked in a sleep of dreams induced by the Goddess herself. Within the walls and down into the very heart of Teamhair, all the occupants, including servants, musicians and minor Kings and Queens all drifted into sleep. Only Francach and The High King remained awake. Francach watched as one by one the people within the Great Hall slumped forward, resting their heads on the tables, or just slid to the floor, curled up like sleeping babies.

"What in the name of Balor is happening now?" screamed Francach. "Guards, guards," he cried, as he jumped to his feet.

Francach looked around at all the sleeping people then glanced toward the King ... he was still awake, yet obviously unaware of what was before him. Drugs, somebody has drugged the mead, he then started moving between the sleeping bodies, kicking a few as he went, and lifting drinking vessels and sniffing at the contents. By now he was sweating like a boar in the chase and his black hair stuck to his face giving the impression that he completely insane, which of course he was, well maybe not completely? He drew his sword and headed for the nearest exit but the door was locked. "The keys; who's got the blasted keys?" he shrieked. He bent down and began to search the guards but couldn't find the keys. In his rage he began to strike the heavy oak doors with his sword, shouting and screaming as he did so. Eventually, his strength left him and he sank to his knees breathing as heavy as a horse that had just ran from Munster in the south to Ulster in the north.

"Guards," he called, but this time the word flowed from him like a whimper.

Raising his head he looked at the big door before him.

"That's not possible," he mumbled through quivering lips, his eyes were as wide as plates as he stared disbelievingly at the massive door. There wasn't a mark on it. No sword marks, no gashes, no stab marks, nothing.

"This damned place is bewitched," he wailed as he looked over at Fionntan. "Who is doing this, tell me or I'll remove your head right now?" threatened Francach. But the king just continued to slump in his seat to all intents and purposes, unaware of the events taking place.

Slowly, Francach rose to his feet and looking around and said, "We've been found out, who could have known, I never told anyone? Spirit, you have betrayed me you devious wretch," he spat.

"Francach, you really are an idiot," whispered the spirit, "I did not betray you, your stupid pride has betrayed you, you are to blame for our demise, you, you, you. Anyway, I see no reason to stay here with you, you may not be able to pass through doors, but I can," the spirit quipped.

"Treacherous weasel," hissed Francach, "I will sort this out myself ... I don't need you, be off."

Before the spirit could remove itself from Francach, another spirit, a more powerful spirit passed through him sending him crashing onto the table that was just behind him.

Arghhhh! He screamed, as he held his throat, and he started to wrench and cough violently. Turning and kicking he fell from the table and on hitting the floor a thing that resembled a cat's fur ball was coughed up and onto the straw decked surface.

"Francach, you imbecile, what have you done to me?" squealed the spirit.

Francach at first looked horrified and then began to laugh.

"You promised me wealth and power and look at you, you

are no more powerful than something a stable boy sweeps out after the horses have left. I'll teach you, you little rodent."

Francach looked around for his sword and raising it, he brought it down fast and hard on the 'thing' that was previously the evil and conniving spirit. The 'thing' split open and revealed a writhing, wriggling ball of what looked like maggots. Francach looked down in disgust and stepped back, and reaching out for the oil lamp nearby, he crashed the lamp spilling the oil over the 'thing' on the floor. He then took a lighted taper and ignited the oil destroying the disgusting thing that wriggled and writhed before him. Once he was sure that the 'thing' was no more, he turned and was confronted by a large figure of a man with a sword in his hand, for the spell had been broken.

"My lord, it's so good to see you looking so well and on your feet again," stammered Francach.

Fionntan High King of Éirinn faced his champion, " Francach, your heart is as black as the shirt on your back, and between you and that worm of a spirit you have all but destroyed this beautiful land, well, now it's over you treacherous dog."

Both men eyed each other.

Francach reached for a cup of mead from the table, and drinking its contents, threw the cup to one side of the hall, and wiping his mouth on his sleeve he looked the King in the eye, "I'll be the one to say when this is over." He laughed confidently. "In less than an hour tributes will begin to arrive for the High King, 'me', the new High King, I will dispatch you to your forefathers, the rest of the Gaels will perish soon after and this land will once again belong to my people, the Fomorians. I don't need a bag of maggots to make me High King, I can do that myself."

With that said, Francach launched his attack. Fionntan stepped back and parried the blow. The Fomorian now slashed wildly at the King, and at the same time reached into his belt for his trusty Scian Dubh with his left hand. The King blocked every blow and thrust that Francach rained down on him, but it was only when they got close did Fionntan see the Scian Dubh in the Fomorians left hand. Quickly, the man in black thrust the knife but it only went through the Kings outer jacket. Fionntan spun into the lunge, drawing his opponent towards him and in one movement hit the Fomorian full in the face with his sword guard. Francach staggered back and fell over the burnt remains of his spirit accomplice. Slipping on the oily stone floor, he wiped the blood from his nose and growled like a wounded beast. Raising his sword high he launched another attack, but this time Fionntan moved to the side and brought his sword diagonally across the Fomorians intended sword arc. Francach could not avoid the blow, and the king's sword sliced through his black coat opening his clothing and revealing a wound to his chest. Francach stumbled backwards, and then straightened himself.

"You think a flesh wound will stop me Fionntan, your wrong. Now you've had your fun, I will slice you into dog meat and still have time to enjoy my dinner before your soul has had time to get back to the halls of your fathers."

"You talk too much traitor. If you want to die in this hall come forward and I will dispatch you back beneath the Sea of Alba from whence you came."

With that there was a mighty clash of steel against steel as Fionntan sprang forward. So furious was Fionntan's attack that Francach reeled backwards falling over the sleeping Captain of the Guard who was laying there. Fionntan raised his sword ready to deliver the final blow, and then stopped.

Francach was looking up at him with eyes wide open and a look of total surprise on his face. There was blood trickling from the corner of his mouth and the sound of his breathing was laboured and noisy. Although the sword had fallen from his grasp and because he had only received a flesh wound to the chest, Fionntan was reluctant to get too close to the wicked scoundrel, for it could be a Fomorian trick. The King stood watching him for what seemed an eternity but he never moved. Francach's Scian Dubh lay at his feet and the King picked it up and slipped it into his belt. Fionntan moved towards the body of Francach and took hold of his lapels to lift him, when suddenly the Fomorians hands came up and gripped the King around the throat. Francach was spitting blood and cursing as he tightened his grip on Fionntan's throat. The Fomorian was grinning and frothing like a mad dog when he suddenly let go and fell back. In Fionntan's hand was the Scian Dubh, its blade covered in the blood of the Fomorian. It was finished; the man in black appeared to be dead. Apparently killed by his own blade? His body was removed sometime that day, possibly by an accomplice and taken back to the sea where he belonged.

Outside of Teamhair, and unknown to the High King, a long procession of tall elegant people was taking place. A massive circle was being created that aligned with the twenty-seven standing stones that encircled the Hill of Teamhair. When the Danann warriors were in place, the Druids walked slowly around the circle attaching a Corn Dolly and Sun Wheel to each of the Stones in turn.

"Cathal, Cathal, what are we doing?" puffed Lulach, who was pretty much out of breath.

"We are doing this because we have been asked to do this," retorted Cathal. "Are you going to question Danu?"

"No." Answered Lulach; feeling a little foolish.

"Then just get on with it."

Just then they both became aware that someone was behind them, and turned.

"Master Druids, still having difficulties are we?" quipped Eóghann.

"No, no, we're fine, just fine … nearly finished," piped Lulach, wiping rain from his face, "Just fine."

Eóghann turned to Orla chuckling, "I love these Gaels, they're so imperfect."

Orla gave him a black look and he coughed, "Sorry. I had forgotten you are a Gael"

"Come, let's do what we came to do," Orla commanded in a very self confident manner which took Eóghann by surprise. It was obvious that Orla was no longer the shy young girl he had earlier encountered in the Village of the Salmon.

"The time of the Solstice is now," she called, "it is, and as always been a time of endings and beginnings, a time of the new replacing the old, but it is a time of awareness in the never-ending cycle of life and death, day and night and summer and winter. You all know what to do?"

When the circle was complete with everyone in their positions and the Corn Dollies and Sun Wheels had been attached to the Standing Stones as instructed, Orla stepped forward facing the main stone with the imprint of a hand in it. To her right stood Eóghann and to her left the Goddess Danu herself. With a deep breath and wiping the steadily falling rain from her eyes, Orla, wrapped in her blue cloak stepped forward and placed her hand into the indentation in the stone. The Danann's raised their magical weapons and the whole of Teamhair began to tremble. The Standing Stones moved like loose teeth, and began to glow and hum with a deep resonance; the wind began to howl like a pack of wolves on the night of the full moon. The main stone was illuminated in a bluish light and one by one; the other stones were lit as if by the first. The ground beneath their feet rose and subsided like a living, breathing being. The noise became intense as the Danann weapons began to glow and pulsate, and as if orchestrated, they released their weapons and they began to rotate like a giant floating wheel. The energy was terrifying and a powerful vortex was being created within the Stone Circle and above Teamhair. Lightning flashed and great clashes of thunder bounced off the far away hills, the valley rattled with the sound. The vortex grew in size and density and it peaked so high it literally went up and up through the clouds and into the sky above. Just then the sun broke through and there was a loud cheer as the golden rays were the first to fall on Éirinn for many a month.

Eóghann looked at Orla. Her hand was still attached to the Standing Stone and she was shining as bright as the stone itself. He glanced over towards Danu who was watching very intensely. She turned her gaze towards Eóghann, sensing his anxiety and smiled. A voice in his head reassured him and he relaxed.

The clouds broke and blue sky could be seen. Within minutes the suns heat began to warm the land and the whole hill became shrouded in a white warm mist. The temperature began to noticeably rise and the sun came through, constant and warm burning the mist off the hill and rolling it into the valley. For the first time in months the land appeared to be happy. The trees and the bushes looked taller and wider. Animals were appearing, bird song could be heard; even the Druids had stopped bickering and had their arms around each other. Ceana, who had not danced in years, embraced Oisian and Coinneach and jigged a little jig to the amusement of Brighde who was clapping her hands like an exited child. Cathal sat on the now dry grass and laughed at the antics of the High Druid Council and thought that nobody will believe this in years to come. Lulach had found his Danann beauty and was lost in conversation and excitement. I have heard from a very reliable source that Lulach was one of the last Druid Bards to travel repeatedly to the Otherworld; well that's what I heard. It was said that he played his Harp so well that the Danann's adopted him as one of their own, and to this day his tunes can still be heard when the conditions are right across the plains of Teamhair.

Orla lay sprawled on the grass with Eóghann and a Danann standing close by.

"Don't touch her," called Danu, "She is filled with earth energy and she will come around if you give her some breathing space."

With that the Danann stepped back leaving Eóghann to watch over Orla. Eóghann looked up at Danu and asked, "Lady, what is to happen to Orla now this work is finished?" Danu looked lovingly towards the girl wrapped in blue, "She will become great in Éirinn, and even when I am forgotten her name will live on in the people of the Gael. She will return to her village and she will take maidens into her care. She will teach them all that is good and wholesome, they will become healers of animals and people alike. They will learn the skills of the earth, how to harmonise their lives with her who gives life to all. They will learn secrets and science, they will read the stars and the seasons and they will become wise. She will become known as 'The Brighde', and she will pass on that title to whoever follows her. She will start a fire that will burn in remembrance of me, but importantly, she will place a flame in the hearts of people that will never be extinguished, in fact Eóghann, she will become the most beloved in Éirinn. We, Eóghann are soon to be replaced by another, yet we have learned that through the cycles of time, our time will come again. Until that time arrives, we, the old ones, along with our children the Danann's, will sleep and rest in our halls until our time returns. Sleep well Eóghann, or should I say Oenghus Mac Og of Brugh Na Bóinne."

With that Danu, Goddess of the flowing waters disappeared and has not been seen for many a year, although having said that, it is said she travels the land occasionally watching over her folk and waiting for her children to need her again.

Book Two

Another Spring Day

"It's been almost thirty summers since Éirinn was healed, and I remember those days like they were yesterday. I still live in the same small village I was born in, but much has changed over time, mostly for the better. My older sister Orla, who we now call Brighde, visits occasionally with some of her students, mainly at festival times, but normally life continues in the village of the Salmon just as before. I get to daydream a lot now-a-days, especially when I'm alone with just the breeze and the pleasant sunshine to keep me company.

My husband Ròidh and son Sionn work the smithy since Branan, my father died, which leaves me with plenty of time on my hands. Gràinne my mother, you remember my mother don't you? Well, she died last winter. It came as no surprise for she had been ill since the time of the great rains all those seasons ago, plus she kind of gave up after father went to the halls of our ancestors. Me? Oh, I'm fine, just the usual aches and pains that come with age, that's when I come to this place near the river and sit in Lugh's warmth watching the children play. Did I tell you I've got three daughters? Oh yes, growing up strong they are. Niamh, Una and little Orla, it's funny, we still call her little Orla even though she's fifteen summers old and she's taller than my older sister who she was named after. They are up there on the hill watching the sheep as we speak. I used to be able to see them from here, but just lately my eyesight is not what it was and I have difficulty spotting them on the tops. Still, I have no need to worry about them; they are sensible young lassies and besides young Brian is with them. Niamh, my other daughter, she's the one that went away when she was nine summers old with a couple of the other girls to learn from big Orla, you know, Brighde, and although she came back a couple of times within the thirteen cycles of the moon, she has changed from child to woman and learned to walk with the grace of a deer in no time at all. That's why I'm sat here now; Niamh is home and is doing the tasks that I would normally do. She said that I should sit above the river and watch the children play, enjoy the smells and sounds of summer and relax, I have to laugh, she said it would do me good, and she was right."

This is my telling;

"Keep the fire as hot as possible Sionn;" instructed Ròidh from across the forge, "I'll make sure that the tub is filled with water for when the wheel rims are ready."

Sionn flexed the whole of his body into the bellows until the fire danced the familiar orange and blue flame. The wheel rims locked by rivets glowed in the fire, and at precisely the right moment Ròidh lifted the rims from the flames with metal grips, and between the two men they quickly fitted the glowing rims to the wooden wheels. Steam and smoke filled the smithy as father and son sank the completed wheels into the bath filled with water. The smell of singed wood and the sounds of contracting metal filled the air as the two perspiring men sat back and looked across at each other through the haze.

"Another job well done father," smiled Sionn.

"We'll take a break and then fit the new wheels on the cart. Come on, let's wash up and see what's for lunch," replied Ròidh clapping his dirty hands together.

The two men walked in through the door of the round house to the smell of fresh bread and hot stew.

"Sorcha, are you there?" called Ròidh as he walked past the hearth.

"I'm here father," called out Niamh, "I've packed the food

into a basket. I thought it would be nice to eat together outside, as it's such a lovely day."

"Yes, of course, where's your mother?" enquired Ròidh looking around.

"She's down by the river ... watching the children," replied Niamh, passing the basket to Sionn who attempted to peek under the linen cloth covering the food.

"Not yet big man," snapped Niamh, with the tone of a learned authority.

"Easy to see where she gets it from," teased Sionn, referring to 'aunt' Orla.

Niamh ignoring the flippant comment and readied herself for the short walk.

"Come on you two, or we'll never eat, lead the way Niamh," Ròidh intervened with a laugh.

As the three walked down the animal track towards the river, the sounds of water and children could easily be heard.

"The tides turned father," Niamh spoke.

The two men looked at each other with puzzled expressions.

"How do you do that Niamh?" called Sionn, has he changed the basket into his other hand.

"What?" enquired Niamh?

"You know, that sort of all knowing thing," mocked Sionn playfully.

"Lucky guess I reckon," laughed Ròidh, winking at Niamh.

As they neared the place where Sorcha was sitting, they looked and noticed that the children had left the river and were making their way up the hill towards them. Sorcha hadn't seen them for she slept peacefully in the warm breeze and sunshine.

"Niamh! Niamh!" cried the leading boy loudly, who arrived first puffing and panting. "There's someone in the water ... we think you should see."

By now other children had reached the adults and were

confirming the find in confused childish breathless chatter.

"Quiet children," Niamh lifted her voice gently above that of the children. "Let me see what all this fuss is about."

The children fell silent.

Niamh raised her hand to her forehead revealing the coiled intertwined serpent tattoo that identified her as a Priestess of Brighde, and shielding her keen eyes from the suns glare, she looked across the bay and scanned the water and sure enough there was something in the water.

Aodh, the first boy to arrive was given the responsibility of leading the children back to the village. Some of the children sighed quite loudly and wanted to stay and see what was happening, but Niamh who was not very tall, raised her shoulders and hands slightly enhancing her stature and smiled inwardly as the children stepped back and began to follow Aodh up the hill, back towards the village.

Sorcha, now woken on hearing the noise came across blinking in the strong sunlight, and approached her husband Ròidh.

"What's happening, what's all the noise about?" questioned Sorcha, gripping his arm rather tightly.

Both men looked at Niamh.

"We must go down to the waters edge and see what the children have seen," responded Niamh, "Come make haste ... leave the basket here ... come, hurry."

Wave Cutter

Wave Cutter

Out on the horizon and beyond normal vision sailed the 'Wave Cutter', a ship and crew so beautiful in form that it was obvious that this vessel was not of this world. She sliced delicately and silently through the waves creating hardly a ripple, so wondrously designed was her hull. Her large double sails bellowed as the wind filled the gossamer canvas pushing her forward in a smooth straight line. The seamen on board were tall and fair of face and they worked the ship as if she was a part of them. So strong was their link with the ship, that to the eye of a mere mortal the ship became a living entity, the sea was its blood, its sails breathing like lungs and the crew its physical moving parts.

"Captain, one of the crew is missing, Drostan hasn't been seen since the last watch," informed the wide-eyed sailor.

The Captain turned to the sailor and enquired about the tide.

"The tide is turning as we speak, but for the last several hours it has been running strongly eastbound."

"This means that there is every chance that the tide has taken him ashore", cried the sailor.

"Or he is gone," the Captain said gravely. "We must wait until nightfall before we venture within seeing distance of the shore, we cannot afford to be seen by the mortals, turn the 'Wave Cutter' around … but maintain our current distance from Éirinn."

"Aye, Captain," barked the sailor as he turned to leave the cabin.

"And double the watch, I want that sailor back …" called out the Captain as the cabin door closed.

The Captain leaned against the inside of the door and sighed, he didn't like deceiving his crew this way, but in this case it was necessary.

Within the hour and with the light fading fast, the Captain of the 'Waver Cutter' came on deck and gathered his men around him. Assuming that everybody was aware that one of their own had gone missing, he began to remind them of the pact that had been made many years before with the Gaels of Éirinn. After many years of conflict, the Gaels and the Danann's had agreed that the 'Overland' would belong to the Gaels, and the 'Underland' would belong to the Danann's. This agreement did not include the seas however, but for the sake of protocol it was concluded that the Danann's would become invisible to the eyes of mortal men and should therefore remain hidden from the physical world.

It appeared that all the men aboard the 'Wave Cutter' understood the implications, and as a man nodded in agreement.

"We must not be seen," impressed the Captain, "Therefore we must sail behind the magical mist that will be created by our Druids ... does everyone understand?"

"Aye, Captain," called the men with one voice.

"Dismissed, and keep your eyes open," responded the Captain deceptively as he turned again in the direction of his cabin.

"Oh, before I go below," whispered the Captain to the Watch Officer, "Send Mordag to me, I need to speak with her."

Impossible

By the time they reached the water's edge, the body in the water had drifted almost to the shoreline. Ròidh and Sionn stopped dead at the water's edge staring at the body floating face down. Niamh rushed past them into the foaming water.

"He could still be alive ... pull him out, quickly," snapped Niamh.

The two men stepped into the cool Celtic waters and grabbing the man's clothing, pulled him towards shore and up onto the sand and pebble beach.

Niamh kneeled down beside him and turned him over. The men stood transfixed, and Sorcha who by now had caught up, panted, "Oh my, he's so young ... is he dead Niamh?"

Niamh lifted an eyelid and in astonishment gasped.

"He's alive; Sionn, father, lift him up, we must take him back to the village where I can treat him."

The two men raised the limp body and began the gentle climb towards the village.

"Who is he, where do you think he came from?" enquired Sorcha, "Is he dangerous, perhaps he's a raider ... his friends may miss him and come back for him."

There was an element of fear in her mother's voice and she was clinging and pulling Niamh's sleeve, demanding some kind of an answer.

"It's fine mother, he's not dangerous, and he is certainly not an enemy," comforted Niamh.

Sorcha went quiet for a while.

"Perhaps we should tell the Druids, Niamh," Sorcha responded a little panicky.

"Mother, it isn't necessary to tell anyone, he's just a young man who's fallen into the sea and got into difficulties. He'll probably be fine in a day or two, and then he'll be on his way."

Sorcha appeared satisfied with that, and Niamh turned to continue up the path. The two men had stopped on hearing the two women speaking, and as Niamh approached she looked to the ground as she passed the two men. She may have convinced her mother with that explanation, but she could feel Ròidh's eyes watching her, for he was anything but convinced. Taking a deep breath, Niamh straightened herself up, and raising her chin she walked with the confident grace of a Priestess of Brighde hoping that this would remove all doubts, and probably make her explanation more feasible.

Ròidh smiled at the confidence of his daughter ... so in control, or so it seemed.

As the group approached the village gates, a crowd had gathered on hearing the news. Aodh was at the front, he must have told everyone. A gap opened up as Niamh led the group into the village. Men bowed in respect and women made a blessing sigil in the air as the Priestess approached. Niamh realised that she would have to allay any fears if this incident was to be kept quiet. She suddenly stopped and turned to face the villagers.

"My people, it is not very often that something out of the ordinary happens here in our village."

This brought a ripple of laughter from the small crowd.

"It's not very interesting to have to pull a drowning man from the sea," said Niamh seriously. "I would however like to inform you that this young man is probably a traveller or even a fisherman from a neighbouring village who got into difficulties."

Many of the villagers nodded at the probability of this being the case, knowing that the sea currents can be treacherous, especially off the coast of Éirinn when the tide turns, or when the moon is full.

"Take him inside father, and place him close to the fire, we must raise his temperature."

The crowds' interest now satisfied they quickly went back to the chores and chatter that villagers occupy.

The two men did as they were requested, and Sorcha following them inside pointing to the cot closest to the warm fire.

"Ròidh, place him there and I'll cover him. Looking up at her husband she asked, "How can a man that has lay in the sea still be alive, I thought that was impossible?"

"I don't know Sorcha, you'll have to ask Niamh, I do believe she knows the answer," answered Ròidh, looking down at the beautiful clean-shaven face of the man in the cot.

Draoi Craft

Three wizened men stood on the bow of the Wave Cutter and, with arms open wide began singing a song that has long since been forgotten in the world of mortal man. From a distance it appeared that a sea mist was rolling across the waves, when in fact, it was the Wave Cutter gliding elegantly over the briny waters shrouded in a magical ethereal haze. It would have been difficult at a hundred paces to see the ship on a clear day, but hidden from the gazing eyes of man by a supernatural fog ... the ship was invisible.

"Maintain the course," issued the captain to the first Officer, "And keep your eyes open."

Just then Mordag came to the captain's door.

"Captain, you wish to see me?"

"Yes, come in and close the door, we have need to talk," said the captain.

Mordag, a tall and intelligent young woman with striking features and eyes the colour of amethyst raised an eyebrow.

Mordag stepped into the captain's cabin and sat near to the captain's table. The captain seated himself opposite and sighed. There was a long pause before he spoke; it was as if he was searching for the correct words. Mordag shifted uncomfortably.

"Mordag," whispered the captain leaning forward, "We have a situation and I might require your services." The captain coughed, nervously playing with a pocket compass. "As you are aware Mordag, we have an agreement with the mortals that we cannot afford to break, or even appear to break. This is what the crew have been told, a member of our crew has gone missing, and we have no idea exactly when, where or why he became separated from the ship. I have spoken with his officer and he reports that the boy was happy and contented aboard the Wave Cutter ... so they assume he has fallen overboard somehow."

"That my dear Mordag; is what I told the crew."

Mordag sat back in her chair and exhaled.

"What they don't know is, is that the missing man Drostan, is in fact Drostan, son of Ross and that his disappearance is a cover."

"Captain, I thought that the missing man was a sailor, are you telling me that this man Drostan, is Drostan the son of Ross the King?" questioned Mordag, sitting forward in her chair.

"Yes," replied the captain.

"Why?" cried Mordag?

There was a momentary pause and then the captain began to reveal the reasons for Drostan being on board his ship.

"Drostan has a request to put before Conn the high King of Éirinn", revealed the captain. "The Danann Druid council and King Ross have knowledge that in the near future, Éirinn will become overrun and her sacred treasures will fall into the hands of invaders, and that my dear Mordag, cannot be allowed to happen. Lulach the Druid, who lives in our realm, came from the mortal world and handfasted a Danann woman. He has lived as one of us for many seasons and is trusted by all. He has been chosen by our Druid council to assist Drostan in Éirinn. In fact, Lulach is aboard and is in full knowledge of events. Mordag, I want you to work with Lulach to liaise with the prince and help him complete his assignment."

There was a long silence before Mordag spoke.

"Captain, I know Lulach the Druid. He spent many winters with us as a guest of my father Fearghas. My father sits on the Druid council and is the Wizard of the ancient portals; I know that Lulach had learned much from my father, and that Lulach is the right person to accompany Prince Drostan."

There was another lengthy silence, and the captain moved uncomfortably.

"I need to know," began Mordag, "My being on board the Wind Cutter appears to be more than just a coincidence."

Mordag turned quickly and gave the captain a steely glance. "I think it's time to tell me what is going on here. Was the disappearance of Drostan planned beforehand? Why was Lulach sneaked aboard ship and hidden from the crew and me, why am I here? I was told this was nothing more than a short sail across the ocean ... out of sight of mortals."

Suddenly, the captain butted in, and holding up his hands, palms outwards, he nervously continued, "Mordag, you have your father's vision and guile. I can however tell you this; Drostan's vanishing was no accident. We must maintain the allusion to the crew that one of our own has been lost, therefore, I ask of you not to mention any of this to anybody. There is only myself and the Watch Officer who know that you are here, I will have a word with him and after that, he will say nothing."

"My father always says that it is wise to know your friends, but is an advantage to know your enemies, captain, who are the invaders that threaten Éirinn?" asked Mordag.

The captain stalled for a moment and then beckoned her to come closer.

"Fomorians, they are gathering a mighty army under the sea betwixt Éirinn and Alba, and according to our information, they will be ready within weeks ... Mordag, the Danann's and the Gaels have maintained a peace for a very long time. It is a peace based on agreements, honour and word of mouth. Éirinn thrives because of a code of integrity, dignity, and cultural pride; the Fomorians would destroy all of that. Mordag, your father knows about this and he chose you above all others because you have the Draoi craft and between you and Lulach, you will know what to do."

"He never said," whispered Mordag, staring into empty space.

"Who!" asked the captain?

"My father," responded Mordag, looking slightly confused.

"He couldn't," responded the captain.

"Lulach is in the cabin next door, will you work with him and …? But before the captain could finish Mordag broke in.

"Yes! I will work with him."

"Good," said the captain as he raised himself from his chair.

He walked to a small alcove and drew back some heavy crimson curtains, and there in the shadows was a small door. The captain tapped lightly on the door and Lulach came through into the light.

"Greetings my dear Mordag, I am so pleased that you have agreed to offer your skills to this adventure, by the way, my wife Banbha sends her love and best wishes … shall we be off. Captain, is it time?" chirped Lulach.

The captain stepped towards the back of the cabin where the window is situated and pulled upon a secret lever. Silently a door opened revealing the outside, a small craft sat below bobbing up and down on the foamy water. The boat had a single gossamer sail almost invisible to the naked eye, and a small sea coloured cover to keep one dry and unseen.

"All you have to do," said the captain, "is push off from the side and allow the Wind Cutter to glide ahead, you'll be out of the mist and then you can make towards the shore. Oh! And don't be concerned about the little boat, it will return to the 'Wave Cutter' like a child to it's mother."

The captain frowned and with a pat on Lulach's shoulder added, "Good luck my friends … Drostan knows what to do."

Drostan

Someone placed another slice of dry peat on the fire and a puff of woody smoke raised itself up like a curling dragon towards the central hole in the thatched roof. A few birds fluttered high on the roof supports bringing down a little dust.

Drostan lay in the cot with eyes closed and felt a few particles touch his face, and although his senses were alert, he never moved a muscle, he had to be sure he was safe and he certainly didn't wish to draw attention to himself.

"How's that young man feeling now ... is he feeling any better?" enquired a voice from outside.

"Aye, he'll be fine I reckon,' answered a deep voice. "He's sleeping at the moment, Niamh is with him."

Drostan having listened to the conversation outside turned his attention to the movements inside. The noises appeared to come from the other side of the hearth. He opened an eye. He could just make out a figure moving around in the dim light behind the fire.

"Good day master mariner, are you hungry?" came a woman's voice, soft and warm.

At first Drostan became a little disorientated and confused, there was no way that the person across the hearth could have seen him open one eye, perhaps there was more than one person in the round house?

"Don't be shy, I know that you have woken, in fact, I know that you were never really asleep," came the voice from within the shadows.

Drostan cleared his throat.

"How, how could you know that I was," There was a long pause, "Feigning sleep?" whispered Drostan. "And yes."

"Yes, what yes?" retorted the voice.

"I am hungry," Drostan's voice now sounded almost

childlike.

Niamh laughed and came out of the dimness. Drostan sat up at the sight of this young woman before him, and asked enquiringly, "How did you know?"

Niamh came closer with a bowl of stew, some fresh bread and a cup of refreshing spring water.

"Here, take this," she reached out and passed him the food and drink and in doing so revealing her intertwining dragon tattoos on the inside of her forearms.

"Lady, I apologise for my deception," he said with a little more respect now.

"Hush, eat your food, we can talk afterwards."

Drostan quietly ate his fill and sat there feeling the strength returning to his limbs.

"My name is Drostan," he said to the young woman sitting by the fire, trying to sound as friendly as possible.

"Niamh, my name is Niamh," she replied.

Both persons smiled at each other as the formalities were satisfied.

Niamh was the first to react. "What were you doing in the estuary, Drostan?

Drostan went quiet for a while, thinking what he should say without giving away his real purpose for being here.

"I'm not from this area," he started, hoping to give some cock and bull story that country folk would swallow.

"I know who you are, and I know where you're from," responded Niamh.

Drostan went quiet again.

"You don't have to tell me if you choose not to, I won't be offended," said Niamh. "I don't know what's happening here, but if you require my help to get back home, I will help you."

Drostan looked up; his eyes sparkled like semi-precious stones in the firelight looking intensely at Niamh sat opposite.

"Who do you think I am?" asked Drostan.

Niamh rose to her feet, "Don't play games with me Drostan, I knew you were a Danann when we pulled you out of the water, you either tell me everything or you tell me nothing. Either way, I will help you home."

Again a long silence, then Drostan spoke.

"Come closer," he beckoned.

Niamh drew closer.

Drostan drew a long breath.

"Can I trust you Priestess?"

Niamh looked down at her tattooed arms and raising her eyes to him replied, "Yes." The word came out like a sacred oath.

"I have to speak with Conn, the High King," whispered the young Danann. "We know of a plot to steal the four magical gifts that we gave to the Gaels in the days of your ancestors."

Niamh stepped back and sat down again.

"I have been sent here by our council to make the treasures safe while Conn gathers his army and defeats an old adversary. If the magical gifts should fall into the hands of those people," He took a deep breath, "Éirinn will be finished and that will be the end of the Gaels and probably my people too. So you see, it is in the interests of us all to secure Éirinn's future." Drostan finished speaking and turned towards the door.

Niamh still wanted more answers, especially how he ended up face down in the sea.

"It was agreed that we would sail within nine waves and that I would jump overboard and walk to the shore, as immortals we cannot drown, so I was to use the cover of the sea to arrive unseen. The enemy has spy's everywhere, and if word gets out that I am here ... I don't have to elaborate, do I?"

Niamh shook her head in response.

"Anyway, our Druids saw some shepherds on the hills overlooking the sea and we decided it too risky to come to close to land and be seen. Ancient treaties have to be observed and protocols must be followed if we were to avoid an incident. I made up my mind to jump ship there and then, unfortunately, I had no idea how far out we were and I became exhausted and passed out. I think that's when you found me."

Niamh got up and filled two drinking vessels.

"Here, drink this it will do you good, I promise you it's not poison," she said with a chuckle, "It's made from honey, but you will know that because you gave the brew to us."

Just at that moment Sionn burst through the doorway.

"Niamh, mother's coming up the path and she's got two strangers with her.

"Oh! You're awake," snapped Sionn, looking over at Drostan. "Feeling better are we?"

"Yes, yes, much better thanks," replied Drostan.

"Good," responded Sionn, "You're not from round here are you, not with that accent anyway. From up north, are we?"

Niamh held her hands up, "No more questions Sionn, it's not the right time, okay?"

"Sure," replied Sionn, looking like a naughty boy.

"What do the strangers look like Sionn?" queried Niamh.

"One's a man and the others a woman," answered Sionn.

"Yes?" Niamh followed, "Tell me more" gesturing with her hands.

Sionn coughed and continued, "Well, the man has the appearance of a Druid and the woman is tall and fair, mother appears to know the Druid as they are laughing and joking with each other." Sionn's voice tapered to almost a whisper, "They're also holding hands."

"Did I hear you correctly Sionn?" Niamh cried.

"Yes, they're holding hands." The young man looked embarrassingly at the floor, his voice squeaking like that of a mouse.

Both Niamh and Drostan looked across at each other, and after a short lull, burst into spontaneous laughter.

Drostan's eyes were beaming, "Friends Niamh, friends have arrived."

The Gathering

Niamh decided to play the diplomat, just to keep the lid on things. It's common knowledge that when important people arrive in a small village, especially twice in as many days, people get nosey and start to ask questions. More often than not though, people begin to put their own interpretation on events if a feasible explanation isn't forthcoming, and before that happens Niamh had decided to satisfy everybody's curiosity.

Stepping out of the roundhouse Niamh walked through the gathering crowd and turned. The people went silent awaiting an expected answer.

"My kinsfolk," she began. "We are honoured to have guests in our village and it would be inhospitable if we did not welcome them with food and drink." Niamh looked at the faces in the crowd. "The young man who is recovering in our home is named Drostan, who had gone swimming and got into difficulties. The people coming up the hill are obviously kinfolk of his and have come to take him home." Again she scanned the faces of the crowd, reading the expressions. "But, before they return home," she began, "Shall we show them what warm and friendly people we are here in the Village of the Salmon." At this the crowd softened and began to clap and call out their approval. Then with a very theatrical sweep of her hands, Niamh proclaimed, "Tonight we will feast and dine in honour of our guests." At this a great cheer of expectation went up as suspicious minds were put at ease. "Gabhran, Donnan, make good the preparations and as the sun slips into her watery bed for the night, we will welcome sister moon and her star children with fires, food, mead and good music." Another great cheer went up and Niamh raised her hands allowing her sleeves to slide down her arms displaying her sacred symbols. "Go my people and make ready," beamed the Priestess, knowing she had created a diversion that no one could possibly object too.

As the people of the village made off to ready themselves and to enthusiastically organise a gathering, Niamh, Sionn and the newly arrived others made their way to Ròidh and Sorcha's home. Once inside Niamh let out a deep breath of relief.

"What was all that about," asked Sorcha rhetorically.

By now Drostan had eaten and drank his fill, tidied up his appearance and was sitting by the hearth.

"Sionn, stand near the door and make sure that no one, not anyone comes within listening distance. Mother, father come closer, Lulach introduce us to your colleague." Niamh spoke, almost whispering.

"Her name is Mordag and she is the daughter of Fearghas," interrupted Drostan with a smile.

Mordag stood and looked over at Drostan, and with a nod of her head proceeded to provide a more satisfying explanation of whom she was, and more importantly why she and Lulach were here.

When she was finished she quietly sat down and Drostan passed her a cup of water as talking is thirsty work in a smoky round house.

For a moment there was a silence while everyone digested what had just been explained.

Next, Drostan gave his version of events, like how he jumped overboard and walked on the sea floor until he became exhausted.

The mortals present were open-mouthed in astonishment at what they were hearing, only Niamh showed no surprise.

Ròidh rose to his feet and explained how the village children had raised the alarm and that they had found Drostan in the sea. Ròidh continued his story until everyone understood that part of the puzzle. Sionn who was popping in and out of the doorway kept calling in agreement, and when people turned to see him, he was gone again.

"I think we have a very good understanding of what has happened here, I think it's now time our good Druid explained why," Niamh said as she stepped out of the shadows and into the fire light.

Lulach coughed, placed his hands on his knees and raised himself up. Firstly, he looked around at all the faces before him and then turned his attention to the door. Sionn had just stepped in. "Sorry, have I?" but before Sionn could finish Lulach continued. "Sionn, stay vigilant, just for a little while longer please."

Sionn nodded, and stepped outside again.

Lulach turned his gaze towards the expectant friends and began his explanation. He told them of the knowledge of the Fomorian threat, the gathering great army under the sea, and the Danann plan to remove the magical treasures to a safe place of keeping until the Gaels dealt with the impending danger.

"None of what we have discussed here is to be uttered to another soul, is that understood?" said Lulach grimly. "Sionn," called Lulach. The young man entered quicker than he had left.

"Yes?"

"Come with me Sionn, I have something to tell you," confided the Druid.

He placed his arm around the young man's shoulders and lead him off into a secluded part of the house, there he informed Sionn of everything.

"Sionn I have told you what I have told the others, secrecy is of the utmost importance, do you understand?" questioned Lulach.

"Yes," the young man nodded, "Yes," he reiterated.

As the sun slipped down over the western sea, people began to gather in the village clearing. The great fires had been lit illuminating the whole area. The aroma of roasting meat and the sweet smell of mead permeated the cool night air; the chattering crowds and the laughter of children gave the atmosphere a peaceful feel. Niamh began to wonder if this party would draw attention from the wrong sort. Still, it was done now and there could be no turning back. Perhaps with a bit of luck they would get away with it … but she wasn't too optimistic. There seemed to be one or two strangers milling around, and that wasn't a good sign.

"So much for keeping it within the village," she thought.

"Is everyone ready," called Niamh, as the group gathered inside the roundhouse.

"We're ready," answered Drostan, looking at the others.

The others nodded in turn.

Niamh beckoned the group closer and whispered.

"Just one thing before we go out and mix with the villagers, stay close together and be careful what you say. There are people out there I have never seen before. Perhaps I'm being overly cautious but it is better to be vigilant especially with so much at stake."

Everybody looked around at each other and then made their way out into the open air.

Within minutes the group were surrounded by the smiling faces of villagers offering them food and drink.

Niamh walked around the area casually chatting with neighbours and friends, yet secretly observing others who appeared to be occupying the more shadowy places. One or two had their heads covered and seemed to be more interested in observing our guests than mixing with the villagers. Niamh made it her business to keep the party together, for she knew there was safety in numbers.

Later that evening as the fires dimmed down and most of the people had left or were curled up asleep, Niamh and Sionn walked around the village area.

"It went well this evening, don't you think?" asked Sionn.

Niamh took a deep breath of the now chill air.

"Time will tell Sionn," She responded, "There were a few strangers in the village earlier," she continued, "Did you notice?"

"You mean the people in the hoods?" answered Sionn.

Niamh nodded.

"They left early, obviously our hospitality is not to their liking," Sionn whispered, looking around for listening ears in the now darkening area.

Niamh smiled at her brother's sense of drama, looked up at the twinkling stars and suddenly said, "Come on, let's join the others."

In the roundhouse the others had pulled their seats into a cosy little circle and were chatting about the evening's events. All agreed that the warmth and generosity of the village had been second to none. Good food, wonderful music, fine mead and an excellent atmosphere had made the night perfect.

"Make room for two more," laughed Sionn as the others shifted positions.

Once seated, all eyes focused on Niamh. She took a cup of warm mead that was offered by Ròidh and scanned each face in turn before speaking.

Lulach smiled to himself because he knew that this was a Draoi technique for drawing people's attention, especially something serious.

"Friends and family," she began in an undertone. "What I have to say is of the most importance … so listen carefully. It appears that our guests have drawn attention from people we must assume are our enemies."

The circle shifted nervously.

She continued, "We have to have a plan to get Drostan to Teamhair and the high King. To go through the forest will be fraught with danger. The main roads will be watched and the open lands of the Burren are too accessible. Any ideas?"

There was a long silence as the little group contemplated the best course of action to take.

"We could travel at night," chipped in Sionn. "We've less chance of being seen at night."

"True!" said Ròidh, "but any group travelling together even at night will easily be seen or tracked."

Sionn looked disappointed that his idea wasn't accepted.

"No, it's a good idea," interrupted Lulach. "We must travel at night, but we must split up into small groups. That way we can create a diversion and lessen our odds at being caught."

Lulach continued, "Someone will have to stay behind and give the impression that we are still here, at least until we have a day or two between us and whoever is watching the village."

"I have an idea," whispered Sorcha.

Everyone fell immediately silent, as this was completely and totally unexpected.

"Mother," exclaimed Niamh, "please, say what you wish to say."

Ròidh looked over at Sionn with an amused look on his face, expecting Sorcha to say something trivial.

Sorcha coughed to clear her throat.

"We need a diversion, yes? " Everyone nodded. Sorcha looked around at all the faces staring up at her. "Where is the best place Sionn to hide a sheep?"

Sionn looked up in surprise.

"Er, in a cave," spat Sionn, thinking that was a good answer.

Niamh sprang to her feet. "Mother, you are so clever."

The others looked totally confused.

"Don't you see," blurted Niamh. "What mother is saying is that if you wish to hide a sheep, the best place is to hide it within the flock."

Lulach looked over at Sorcha and gestured her to continue.

"High on the hill overlooking the Village is an ancient rock carving of our Earth Mother. We will invite all our cousins from the surrounding villages to celebrate and visit the site, offering gifts to the Earth Mother for a good harvest for the coming year. We could organise this for say, three days time. That will give us time to prepare for our little escape, and for the villagers to organise themselves for the short journey. It will mean that about three hundred people will be here, and we can easily hide ourselves within that number unnoticed by prying eyes and calculate our escape somewhere along the route."

Sorcha sat down looking a little timid and somewhat embarrassed at her own boldness.

There was a long silence along with a few shuffling nervous feet.

"Brilliant, absolutely brilliant," exclaimed Mordag jumping upright, her Danann accent thick and musical.

Green Man

The House in the Forest

Word went out to the surrounding districts that a celebration to the Earth Mother would take place in three days time, and offerings and supplication would be made for a successful harvest. Within hours, people began to arrive in the village and great joy and happiness was experienced when family and friends met for the first time for many months. Little children were introduced to aunts and uncles also for the first time and great hoops of laughter rose spontaneously when discovering most of the little ones had been named after older family members. The two Danann's watched with great curiosity and were warmed by the affection that the Gaels had for one another. Niamh noticed the changes that came over the little group members as they prepared themselves mentally for the task ahead. Ròidh and Sionn busied themselves in a material way, while her mother got down to repairing torn and old clothes for the journey. Lulach the Druid, Drostan and Mordag sat huddled together discussing how all of this would be presented to King Conn without causing a diplomatic incident. Niamh herself would try to hold everything together, and her skills, she hoped, as a Priestess would be an asset to the group. She poured herself a cup of water and sat down by the hearth, and looked into the fire. The flames danced as the draft caught them and it wasn't long before images began to appear within. A forest and a house revealed themselves. The forest was bright with beautiful trees of all kinds, and there was birdsong that brightened the heart and made one's soul dance with delight. Various animals gathered around the parameter, seemingly unafraid of whoever occupied the house. The house itself was round and flowers grew up its sides, giving the house the impression that it was alive. But as quickly as the image had appeared it was gone again. Niamh sat back and noticed that everybody was looking at her. She jumped to her feet spilling her drink and started to sink as her legs gave way. Mordag was the quickest to react and swiftly covered the space between herself and Niamh. Mordag put her arms around the sinking Priestess and helped her into her seat. Drostan had meanwhile filled her cup with warm mead and herbs and held it to her lips. Niamh drank, a little at first, then big gulps until the cup was empty. The group gathered around her awaiting an explanation.

Sorcha spoke, "Niamh, what happened?"

"I saw something in the flames, a bright forest, a beautiful house, animals, birds and flowers. Sounds so beguiling and wondrous, and within the house a power so intense I felt my spirit leaving my body to be there. That's when I came over all dizzy."

"What does it mean Niamh, is it dangerous?" asked her mother with a worried expression on her face.

"It's nothing," Whispered Mordag. "We all get dizzy sometimes, especially if we look into a fire with dancing flames."

Drostan's confused look said it all. Mordag was not revealing all what she knew.

"Well, I don't like it," said Sorcha. "There's something going on and I don't like it," she repeated.

Ròidh placed his arm around his wife's shoulder and smiled comfortingly.

"I don't like it Ròidh, there's something very wrong," she muttered as they walked away from the group.

Ròidh stopped and turned around. "Niamh is everything okay."

"Its fine father, it's just as Mordag said," Niamh responded.

The group turned away and returned to what they were doing before the incident.

Mordag went outside and was quickly followed by Niamh.

"Mordag!" called Niamh in an undertone.

Mordag stopped but stared straight ahead. Niamh caught up

and walked around to face her.

"Mordag, what happened to me in there?"

"You had a dizzy spell, that's all," replied Mordag not too convincingly.

"Mordag, I need to know the truth, the whole success of this group may rely on me understanding all that is happening."

"I cannot tell you Niamh for I do not know, but there is a small pool off the path to the shoreline. Go there tonight, the sky will be clear and the moon will be close to full. Look into the pool at the moons refection and the answer will be forth-coming."

With that Mordag walked away and spoke no more about it.

As the last remnants of a brightly coloured sundown sank below the western horizon, the stars twinkled and the moon shone bright, the Priestess slipped silently and unseen out of the village. Moving swiftly yet carefully, she made her way down the path towards the silvery sea that reflected the eerie ghostly pale light of the moon, casting strange otherworldly shadows that danced on the rocks and the slightly swaying trees. Occasionally, she thought she heard movement behind her, sometimes to the side, but as she turned to the sound it stopped and she put it down to her imagination and pushed the thoughts from her mind as only a trained Priestess could. As she approached the spot where the pool was, she could see that it really did capture the moon in its reflection, just as Mordag had said. Of course, the art of 'Scrying' was something she had learned as a Priestess, yet this was something different, something much more intense and esoteric. Again she heard a sound and she spun to meet it. Nothing! By now she was becoming spooked and even a trained Priestess can feel fear. Her heart began to beat heavily in her chest, and she could hear her pulse as her blood flowed faster through her veins.

"Calm down, calm down," she whispered to herself.

She turned slowly scanning the near area in the silvery moonlight, paying extra attention to the shadows for any movement that could hide prying eyes. After several minutes of complete silence, her heartbeat began to return to normal as she became satisfied that it was her fears and imagination that was the biggest threat to her safety.

She sat by the pool and took a long deep breath, and staring into the water, swirling images began to appear. Again she saw the house in the forest; the animals and birds, even the sounds that she had heard previously began to ring in her ears. She could see the vines growing up the outside of the house, flowering in a cacophony of colour. Birds were nesting there feeding their young, butterflies and ladybirds and a whole host of other insects could be clearly seen, in fact, the whole house seemed to be alive with nature.

Niamh focused on a small square window opening and very quickly found herself looking into a spacious room. It was light and airy and teeming with all kinds of animals. Oddly, it was as bright inside the house as it was on the outside yet there were no oil lamps or fire within the house. Raising her eyes upwards she gasped. The room had no visible roof for all she could see was blue sky, flying birds and the rays of the sun shining down on the inhabitants within.

Suddenly, the animals all moved to create a clear path from the window to the hearth to reveal what looked like a large green shrub. Niamh stood transfixed as the shrub turned and exposed a smiling face. At once she was drawn into the room and moved across the earthen floor as if riding on air. She now stood before the shrub man who opened his mouth and began to speak.

"Do not be afraid, Priestess, I wish you no harm," spoke the shrub man softly.

Niamh thought his voice sounded like the breeze blowing through the trees in springtime.

"Why are you here?" questioned the shrub man with the same soft tone.

"Answers," replied Niamh. "Although I had no idea that I would intrude on you, and I apologise if I have unwittingly trespassed into your realm."

"I am the one you call the Greenman, lord of the forest and nature, nobody comes to me unless invited ... the fact that you are here obviously means that you have been called here for a reason."

"Yes, I was going to ask you about that," responded the Priestess, now feeling a little more secure now the feeling of danger had past.

The Greenman let out a long sigh, and then with what seemed to take an eternity began to explain to the Priestess why she had been brought before the lord of the forest.

"We know what is happening in Éirinn Priestess," spoke the Greenman, with a rustle of leaves. "Danu is out and about in the mortal world, your world, and she is aware of all that is happening," whispered the lord of the forest. "The Goddess wants me to help you succeed in alleviating the threat to the land that we all, mortals and immortals, love. Therefore, I will give you three magical tools that will assist you in your quest."

"Wait!" blurted the Priestess. "I am not in charge of this - so called quest, I am just a simple Priestess who offered her assistance by mere accident."

"Ha-ha-ha," laughed the Greenman at the irony of her words. "Nether the less, you have been chosen by the Goddess you serve to lead this group and restore peace to the land, above and below." Instructed; the Greenman, and after a very long pause spoke again. "Firstly, I gift you this Silver Horn. When you use it, it will summon all animals to your assistance and you will be able to communicate with them. Secondly, the Rainbow Staff that controls the elements, be very careful for this gift holds terrible power, and lastly, the greatest gift of all, the

Broach of Danu, this will help you change your shape at will."

Niamh was about to interrupt again, for her head was filled with questions that required answers, when suddenly there fell a total silence and instantly there was blackness.

The Priestess opened her eyes to discover that she was lying on the grassy knoll overlooking the pool. She could see by the track of the moon that very little time had passed since she arrived at this spot, yet so much had apparently happened.

"Otherworldly dreams are like that," she thought, not totally convinced of the experience that she had just had.

As she rose to her feet, she felt the movement of something swing on her belt, and looking down she could clearly see a Silver Horn, exquisitely engraved with many animal figures. Then she noticed the beautiful metal Broach attached to her shawl. The metal was reddish in colour and when she was about to touch it, its colour and appearance changed. At her feet lay a wooden Staff, decorated with intricate swirling designs. She reached down and carefully picked it up. As she held it, it changed colour and the clever little designs seemed to move along its length. Turning the staff around in her hand she could see that the symbols representing the directions moved independently, and always pointed to where the desired direction is.

"These were indeed magical gifts. I'm still asleep and dreaming," she thought. "I'll wake up shortly and find that none of this really happened. In the meanwhile, I'll make my way back to the village and back to my bed." She sighed totally exhausted by her ordeal.

Climbing the path seemed much harder than normal and very soon she rapidly began to tire. She was just about to stop and sit down when a female voice commanded,

"Don't stop, keep walking."

The shock stunned the Priestess awake, and she spun to see where the voice had come from, only to see the disappearing shape of a fox melting into the darkness.

"I must have eaten something really odd last night," thought Niamh. "This has got to be the most surreal night I have ever had."

With that she made her way silently back into the village and finally to her bed. She didn't bother to undress for she was exhausted; she just flopped down and immediately fell into a deep, deep sleep.

Book Three

Slipping away

The sun was shining brightly when Niamh woke, and rubbing her eyes, she looked around at an empty round-house. The noise from outside was intense as the milling chattering crowds gathered for the short journey to the site where the Earth Mother celebrations would take place.

"I'm late, I'm late," she blurted, "What kind of an example am I setting?" she thought.

Just then Mordag came in and offered her a cup of spring water.

"I take it your late night caught up with you," she joked.

Niamh just smiled in response.

After finishing her drink, she quickly changed into something more suitable for the journey and readied herself.

"Sit down Priestess," insisted Mordag, "Just for a moment."

Mordag stood over her and offered her some bread and cheese.

"Eat; you will need your strength," pressed the Danann.

Niamh took the food gratefully and began to eat, feeling the energy returning to her limbs.

"Thank you, I feel much refreshed."

Mordag turned towards the door, and without turning back, said, "Come; let's make a start."

There was urgency in her voice and the Priestess responded. Once outside and a few deep breaths of clean air to clear her head, she suddenly turned and rushed back inside.

"My things, I must take my things," she said, rather un-Priestess like.

Drostan looked across at Mordag, who in turn looked across

at the Druid.

"She'll be fine," smiled the Druid, reassuring the two Danann's, and as if on queue, the Priestess popped out of the entrance fully prepared with staff in hand, broach on breast and horn hanging from her belt.

The village soon emptied as the long procession of extended family groups made their way slowly and steadily up the well worn path in the direction of the Earth Mother site. Sorcha, Ròidh and Sionn constantly kept a watch for strangers in the group.

"There are some at the front and some at the back," reported Sionn.

"And I've seen a few figures on the hills above, and scuttling like rodents within the woods," added Ròidh.

It was late afternoon when the long stream of people arrived at the site and they were somewhat surprised to find a series of fires already lit.

The area had been cleaned and prepared for the group, and there was hot clean water and the smell of cooking coming from a very large bubbling cauldron which sat over the central fire.

"There's plenty for everyone so please don't rush forward," called a familiar voice from across the space.

Sorcha rushed forward, "Una, Little Orla, she cried in a very excited, almost child-like way.

"Wonderful," thought the Priestess, and then in a loud voice shouted, "Well done sisters," she chirped, as everybody clapped and voiced their approval.

Soon everyone was seated and sated from the tasty and satisfying food, some; especially the very young and the elderly were lying back and falling one by one silently into sleep.

When all had settled down and family groups became engaged in noisy chatter, Niamh gathered her group together asking her mother, father and her siblings to sit around the group just beyond ear-shot and to politely discourage others from approaching the group. The little band could now speak freely without fear of being overheard.

It had been suggested that the path through the forest might give most cover when making their exit, but Niamh insisted that over the hills and out in the open would be to their advantage. Drostan looked a little perplexed, but Mordag hushed him to his annoyance.

"Who is going with who?" asked Lulach.

"There's been a change of plan my Druid," whispered Mordag.

"What! I thought we had agreed that we would split into groups, and one group would carry out the quest whilst the others became decoys?" questioned Drostan, "We cannot change things now."

"Yes we can," pressured the Priestess. "There has been a change of circumstances Drostan, I'll explain at the first opportunity ... but not now."

There was a long silence as Drostan and Niamh locked eye contact. Drostan eventually nodded and looked away.

"Well, that's settled then. One of my sisters will become Mordag. Aodh from the village can wear Drostan's hood, and Brian the shepherd will become Lulach. Everyone will keep a low profile, not drawing attention to the group or themselves while we, which are, Drostan, Mordag, Lulach and I slip quietly away. Any questions?"

"With you gone, who is taking the ceremony to the Earth Mother?" asked Drostan.

"My aunt Orla, also known as Brighde, she will arrive just before the dawn. She is bringing Raven with her. Raven is about my size and cloaked and veiled she will, to all intents and purposes be me, at least for a few hours at least. The deception will give us time to slip away unnoticed."

Drostan looked totally confused. "How do they know about the plan, you have been with us most of the time?"

The Priestess cast a reassuring smile, "Let's just say we have friends in high places."

Mordag slapped her thigh and chuckled, and with that they all settled down to rest.

As dawn began to break people were waking and the camp was starting to become noisy as children woke, some a little fractious. Many were going off to find some privacy to relieve themselves, whilst others washed themselves in the clear cold waters that tumbled refreshingly down the hillside.

Niamh sat up on her elbows and looked around. Her sisters were busying themselves with making breakfast for the villagers and were being incredibly patient seeing that some of the children were standing around, dishes in hand like hungry wolves. She looked across at Mordag, she was awake but obviously not yet ready to stir. Lulach was still rolled into a ball and snoring loudly. Drostan was missing, probably gone to the privy, she thought. Then she saw him, he was walking towards the old spring, accompanied by two others. As quick as a flash she was on her feet and making her way across the clearing without drawing too much attention to herself.

"Drostan," she called as she drew real close.

All three turned around together.

"Am I glad to see you," Niamh whispered with a broad smile on her face. "How long have you been here?"

Orla, now known as Brighde embraced her sister and fellow Priestess and they hugged each other for several minutes.

"Raven how you have grown my sister," wrapping the young Priestess in a loving embrace.

Niamh looked at the young girls forearms where the symbols of the Priesthood were plain to see. On each of her forearms were the entwined serpents tattooed as a permanent reminder that the office of Priestess is for life. Not all students of the temple get that far, as it will take years of personal dedication, much learning and discipline to become a Priestess of the

Goddess.

"May I suggest you keep your arms covered until we are gone," smiled Niamh. "Nobody must suspect anything or the game will be up before we step foot outside the camp."

The young Priestess tugged on her sleeves and nodded.

"Drostan, I had no idea that you knew my sister," questioned Niamh.

"I don't," said he. "It was she who knew who I was."

Brighde looked across to her sister and winked.

"I should have guessed," smiled Niamh. "Come let's get back to the others and make our plans."

Once back with the group, Niamh reiterated who was doing what, and when. The diversion would be enough to give Drostan, Mordag, herself and Lulach time to vacate the area and start on the road to Teamhair, albeit not the obvious road as that would be watched.

The Sun was now warming the hillside and the night chill had completely disappeared. The crowds were gathering at the foot of the short path that leads to the Earth Goddess carvings, and the two sisters Una and young Orla were organising the people into orderly groups. The people themselves were carrying various offerings to lie at the feet of the Earth Mother. Everybody was excited and there was much noise and movement, perfect for slipping away virtually unnoticed. Drostan, Lulach, Mordag and the Priestess hung back as the crowd moved ever forward.

"Hold hands," whispered the Priestess.

Lulach grabbed Mordag's hand. Mordag reached out to Drostan who took her hand in his, and lastly, Niamh gripped Drostan's other hand.

"Hold on, and don't let go" she said firmly.

The others looked at each other bewilderedly for she had kept this bit to herself.

"I summons the power of the broach of Danu," she cried.

Suddenly what appeared to be a strange green gossamer mist, seemed to surround them all.

"Come, we must hurry," and the four of them made their way across the open hillside and into a small shaded ash wood. From the cover of the trees they could see a line of people making their way up the path to the sacred area, and from here it reminded them of a snake moving slowly up the hill to offer itself to the giver of all life. The symbolism was very powerful and very profound.

"What happened?" asked Drostan.

"I was about to ask the same thing?" chipped in Lulach.

Mordag looked at Niamh without speaking.

"Okay, I'll tell you. What you experienced was the power of the Gods."

"What" exclaimed Mordag?

Niamh made a hushing sound and quietened the group.

"Please, keep your voices down. We may not have been seen as such, but we could quite easily give our position and advantage away by noise."

"Let me briefly explain, or we will be here all night," mumbled the Priestess. "By the power of this Broach we were able to shape shift and therefore escape."

"Shape shift?" blurted Drostan.

"Yes, what people saw as we made our leave was four sheep moving across the grassland. This is sheep country is it not? Nobody would look twice at a few sheep up here," smiled Niamh.

"Brilliant," said Lulach with a chuckle.

"This must look weird from the outside," said Niamh with a muffled laugh. "Four sheep talking to each other, I think we should stop holding hands now and break the spell."

The Greenman Reappears

The group of four made good progress after their unseen escape from the crowd. Travelling north east they soon came to the edge of a small wood. Lulach thought it may be the same wood that he and Eóghann had passed through many years earlier, but he wasn't sure. The mention of Eóghann's name had stopped the group in their tracks, for Eóghann, also known as Oenghus Mac Og was an ascended one and was beloved by Gael and Danann alike.

"Come, we have work to do," ushered Niamh, making a sigil of good intent in the air.

The group moved quietly on through the wood as darkness began to fall. They were all tired by now but none complained for they knew that haste would be their ally, especially at this time.

Suddenly, Niamh put her hand up and the whole troop, which had been walking in single file, came to an abrupt stop.

"What is it?" whispered Drostan.

"Shush," came the response.

The Priestesses arms signalled a downward motion, and the group sank silently down on their knees, making themselves small and difficult to see in the wooded twilight.

Mordag's hearing was the most acute and she was the first to hear the voices of men just in front of them. She signalled to Niamh by pointing in the direction the voices were coming from. The Priestess acknowledged that she understood, and signing to the others to stay still, she edged carefully forward until she had a clear vision of who they were and how many.

Niamh placed her hand on her magical broach and whispered an incantation. Instantly she turned into a moth and flew in the direction of the voices. She was also aware that as a moth she was in mortal danger of becoming someone's snack, especially the bats that are active at this time, so with great care and attention she moved ever closer to the men whose voices she had heard. Once within a few yards of them she settled down on a leaf, spreading out her soft wings and blended into her surroundings.

Watching carefully, she noticed that the men were heavily armed and appeared to be waiting for someone to rendezvous. She also noticed that they had no fire, which meant that they didn't wish to draw attention to themselves from any uninvited visitors that may cross their path. The men were obviously nervous and twitchy as every now and then they would stop talking and peer into the trees, or jump up with hand on sword hilt.

Niamh stayed quite still.

After what seemed a long time, an old woman stepped from the dark shadows. The men, startled, leapt to their feet.

"Identify yourself old woman," called one of the men who was obviously there leader.

After a short pause the woman spoke.

"My name is Mòr and I am from the Druid High Council."

"Step forward so we can see you," spoke the leader of the group.

The old woman stepped forward suddenly straightening up and revealing herself to be a much younger person.

"How do you do that?" asked the leader, stepping backwards in surprise.

"It's not important," said Mòr. "Take me to your King at once, that is the reason why you're here, is it not?"

"Yes, of course, we were just a little surprised to see an old woman. I meant no offence."

"As opposed to an old man, no doubt?" responded the Druidess.

There were a few murmurings of discontent between the group and then they picked up there things and moved off.

Niamh waited until she was sure that they were gone, and touching the magical broach again and with a few supernatural words spoken in an undertone she changed back into her normal self again to the disappointment of the moth eating creatures that pervade the woods at this time of the year.

Quickly, she made her way back to the others who were patiently, yet silently waiting for her return.

"Who was it?" enquired Drostan, looking rather concerned.

"Friend I think;" "Do any of you know a Druid woman by the name of Mòr?"

Blank faces stared back.

"Okay, I'll take that as a no then, shall I?" whispered the Priestess. "Come; let's make haste, if we follow them they will take us to Teamhair, and to the High King."

With that they gathered what little they had, and maintaining silence, they quickly made their way along the little path in single file.

Mòr suddenly stopped and looked back.

"What is it?" asked the leader.

"I thought I heard something," whispered Mòr.

"Probably just a squirrel or something," declared the leader.

"Yes, you are probably right," murmured Mòr as she continued to scan the wood behind them.

Mòr's senses were sharp and she could feel a presence nearby.

"I know your there, whoever you are," she intoned to herself.

She then quickly and unexpectedly turned and set off at a pace down the path quickly followed by the soldiers in hot pursuit.

"By the old Gods whiskers," declared the leader. "I thought we were supposed to be leading her to the King."

One of the other soldiers slapped him on the back and laughed.

"Last one back buys the ale," he chuckled, and then they all set off in pursuit of Mòr.

Back in the trees, about fifty paces away stood Mordag. She had moved faster than the rest and had seen Mòr stop and turn to survey the woods behind.

"She knows we are here," she thought. "We must be extra vigilant if we are to remain a secret."

By now the others had caught up and Mordag told them all what she had seen.

"Where are they now," asked Drostan, who was looking a little weak.

"They have moved off again, I think she's trying to outrun us," offered Mordag.

"If she is from the Druid High Council why would she be fleeing from us?" Lulach chipped in rhetorically.

"I think we should rest and eat," Niamh cut in. "It's not been long since Drostan recovered from his incident."

The others nodded in agreement, although Drostan insisted that he was fine, in reality, he looked exhausted.

Niamh looked up at Mordag. Mordag's keen eyes trained on the path ahead.

"Follow them and leave markers for us to follow you, can you do that?"

"Yes," said Mordag in all seriousness.

"Then follow them and be extra careful for if Mòr truly is from the Druid High Council we have nothing to fear, if not, then we have much to be concerned about. Go! Go fast my Danann friend."

Mordag took a small leather bottle of watered mead and some honey cakes and set off down the path, and very soon the sound of her soft footsteps gave way to silence and once again only the noise of the wood could be heard. Niamh and Lulach looked across at each other and then at Drostan who had fallen soundly into asleep.

"Let him sleep for a while, he needs it," whispered the Bard.

Niamh nodded and said no more.

All three fell into silence and sleep soon followed.

The morning broke with its usual bright sunshine and the early activity of the creatures that live in this wood. The sudden volume woke Lulach with a start.

"Good morning master Bard," came a call from Niamh.

Drostan slept on undisturbed.

"How long have we slept?" questioned the Bard.

"A few hours," said the Priestess. "We can set off as soon as Drostan wakes, we can eat as we go."

Drostan woke about an hour later; the rest had done him good. The colour had returned to his face and when he stood he appeared stronger. The Priestess quickly ran through what was happening and after a long drink of watered mead they took a few honey cakes in hand and set off down the path.

Luckily, with a straight path and good weather the three made good progress. Mordag had indeed left good markers for them to follow which made the way much easier. About mid-day, the path opened up into a small clearing and there at the far side of the clearing and on the floor leaning against a tree was Mordag. Mordag head was slumped to one side. Something was wrong. Something was very wrong.

Drostan went to push passed but Niamh stopped him.

"Stand still and listen," whispered the Priestess.

They stood like statues, but heard nothing but total silence.

"They are waiting for us," said the Bard quietly.

"Yes, I know," responded the Priestess.

"What about Mordag?" said Drostan a little panicky. "Is she injured?"

"Let's get off this path and make ourselves unseen," said Niamh softly.

With that the three held hands and using the broach and a

few magical words, they all transformed into small rodents running through the undergrowth. Within a matter of seconds they were gone. As rodents they could now do things that humans would find impossible, so, Drostan and Lulach hid in a trees root system while the Priestess as a rodent made her way back to the clearing. Once there she circumnavigated the area to where Mordag was, and using her rodent senses could feel and smell that no one was close. Moving slowly and silently she moved behind the tree and noticed that Mordag had been bound to the tree with cord, and looking up she could see that the Danann had blood in her hair and had obviously been knocked unconscious. The rodent rubbed her fur against Mordag's hand. She responded with a twitch. The rodent did it again, and this time Mordag attempted to brush her away. Niamh couldn't chance becoming human again for fear of getting caught, so she started to nibble at the bonds holding Mordag's hands. Mordag again brushed her away.

"Stay still Mordag," said Niamh. "But all that came out of her mouth was a little squeak. There has to be a way of letting her know it's me," thought the Priestess.

Mordag was by now fully conscious, except for a bump the size of a chicken egg on the side of her head. She tugged on her bonds but it was hopeless, they were tight and strong and she was not going to slip from these. She looked around the clearing for the person or persons who had surprised her on the path, but they were apparently gone. Then she saw someone through the trees across the open ground.

"It must be the Druid woman," she concurred.

Suddenly in front of her she noticed a small rodent looking up at her.

"Well, you're a brave little chap, aren't you?

The rodent started to gather small twigs and hurrying and scurrying at a frantic pace spelled out the word 'Niamh' out of the twigs down by her feet.

At once the penny dropped. Mordag dropped her head forward so the woman across the clearing couldn't see her face and said, "I understand, get me out of here."

The little rodent ran behind the tree and bit through the cords that held the Danann captive.

With great speed Mordag rolled over and leaped behind the tree, and in a flash of light Niamh materialised before her, and in one movement wrapped her arms around her and touching the broach and a few very fast words both she and the Danann woman were gone, scurrying through the grass as fast and unseen as possible.

At the time all this was happening, the soldiers were half way across the grassy area and were totally perplexed at the sudden disappearance of the woman.

"Out of my way you oafs," shrieked Mòr. "Where is she, where has she gone ... don't just stand there, look for her, and this time chop off her head."

The soldiers were horrified at the suggestion, but did as she asked for they were under strict orders from King Conn himself to escort the Druid representative and that included service.

By the time the soldiers got back to the clearing and empty handed to boot, they found Mòr kneeling down on the grass before the tree.

One of the soldiers removed his helmet thinking the tree was holy or something.

"I'm not praying, you idiot, look at this and tell me what you think," yelled Mòr.

The soldiers all craned to see what she was looking at.

"Twigs?" asked one soldier who was dismissed with a glare.

"Any dolt can see that they are twigs," spat Mòr. "But what do the twigs say?" She added with venom.

"Ah! We don't do any of that reading stuff, we're soldiers," piped in the leader.

Mòr dismissed that last remark with the disdain it deserved. "It says 'Niamh'," she spat. "What witchcraft is going on here," she murmured.

The soldiers shrugged their shoulders unknowingly.

After some choice words and bad tempered exchanges, Mòr took off down the path.

"Come on, come on," she shouted back. "We don't want to keep the King waiting, do we?"

The soldiers grumbled, lifted their packs and ran after her. Within minutes the sound of rattling, heavily armed soldiers faded into silence, and all that could be heard was bird song and a gentle breeze that fluttered the leaves in the high branches.

Out of the gnarled undergrowth came four little rodents into the filtered sunshine. Instantly there was a whoosh and four people stood blinking and swaying in the bright light.

"I'll never get used to that," mumbled Drostan.

"It does come in handy though," smiled Lulach.

"Lets have a look at your head Mordag," said the Priestess. "My, that's quite a bump you have there," she said as she examined the Danann's head.

She pulled out of her bag a small pot with yellow salve, and applied a little to the wound.

The Danann gave out a little gasp.

"You'll be fine within the hour Mordag, you're a Danann."

The four gathered up their belongings and together started down the track again. This time Drostan volunteered to go on ahead for he too was a Danann, and his sight and hearing was almost as good as Mordag's.

The rest of the journey was fine. There were no more surprises or unwelcome visitations, and within a few hours, the Priestess, the Bard and the Danann woman caught up with Drostan who was sitting cross legged at the edge of the wood looking out over the hill of Teamhair.

"Look, over there ... can you see them?" said Drostan excitedly.

The Priestess and Lulach strained their eyes in the fading sunlight.

"I can see them," said Mordag. "It's our Druid friend and her escort; she's standing and looking back this way, obviously looking for us."

In the background stood the beautiful Caiseal of Teamhair.

Niamh moved them back into wood a little and said," we can sleep here tonight and tomorrow we will enter Teamhair."

The others nodded in agreement and settled down for the night.

Niamh had difficulty sleeping as the thoughts of the days to come preoccupied her mind. "How do we convince the High King to part with his magical treasures, and how do we persuade King Conn that there is a threat to Éirinn?"

She turned over and could see the outline of Teamhair in the darkness.

"What of the Druid called Mòr, what do we say about her?"

"So many questions and not enough answers," she thought.

It was just then that she thought she could hear running water. She looked around at the others and noticed that they all slept soundly. Rising quietly from the ground she made her way to where the sound was coming from. Slowly and carefully she tip toed her way ever closer, and moving aside a branch she saw what looked like a figure.

"Come closer Priestess," spoke the figure with a voice that rang like a harp.

Niamh put her hand on her broach, but then the voice said, "I take it you've used it then."

Niamh moved her hand away and stepped forward.

The figure turned to face her and she gasped.

"My Lord, why are you here."

"I have always been with you, from the day you were born I have been here for you, it's just that you never knew."

"Tomorrow I must convince the High King to part with his treasures, and tell him about the Fomorian threat to Éirinn, how do I do that? I am a Priestess not a honey tongued knight or the like."

The Greenman shuffled with laughter like a bush in the breeze.

"Don't worry Priestess, you have a friend yet unknown and the outcome of tomorrow will not rest with you alone. Your heart will win the day, believe me."

Niamh moved closer and could see that within the branch like arms of the Greenman sat a fawn. At his feet were rabbits and squirrels and other little creatures. Birds sat in his foliage like hair, jumping and chattering. His feet were together and curled up like a large basin and water was running down his trunk like body into it. She moved closer to see what was in there. Swimming within the basin was a large fish, a salmon who on seeing her, came to the surface and looked at her, as if inspecting her.

"So! You are she, are you?" questioned the salmon.

"I don't wish to appear rude, but I've never spoken to a salmon before."

The Greenman groaned.

"Did I say something wrong?" gasped the Priestess.

"No, no. You're doing just fine," said the Greenman. "Let me introduce you to each other shall I? Niamh, Priestess of Brighde, allow me to introduce you to Fionntan, the first creature ever created. Fionntan knows everything and if you ask him politely he will tell what you want to know."

The Greenman sat back with a creak. "Ah! That's better."

Niamh looked at the salmon that was waiting for a response.

"Fionntan"

"Yes?"

"What should I say to The High King tomorrow?"

The salmon splashed around a little and then with a slosh of his tail responded.

"Stand tall before the King and tell him clearly and confidently that you are here to speak on behalf of all Éirinn. Tell him that you speak for the living and the dead and for those yet to come. For the people, animals, trees, and the very Earth herself. Tell him that and he will put things right between the people of Éirinn and the old foe, the Fomorians. King Conn is a good King and he will know what to do."

With that said the image of the Greenman began to fade slowly into invisibility and all around returned to silence. The Priestess looked down at the now empty space on the grassy knoll and there sat a little golden hazelnut. A hushed, yet otherworldly voice like the tinkle of little bells rained softly down from the trees telling her to pick it up, which she did without hesitation and placed it in her little bag that hung from her leather belt. With that done she returned to the glade where the sleeping group were and quietly lying down so as not to disturb the others, drifted gently and peacefully into sleep.

King Conn – High King of Éirinn

The morning broke with the usual sound of woodland noises and a stiff neck through sleeping in an awkward position.

The others slept on undisturbed as Niamh rubbed her neck and thought of what the day would bring. After a few minutes she moved over to a patch of grassy moss and dabbing a cloth on the glistening green to wet it enough to wipe the sleep from her eyes.

"I'll be glad of a bath," she muttered.

"Okay, time to rise," she called loudly and clapping her hands at the same time. "Lets ready ourselves as we have much to do and achieve this day."

Mordag was the first to rise and Niamh noticed that her head was now completely healed.

"Lucky Danann," she whispered under her breath.

Lulach, the oldest of the group sat up on his elbows and looked tired.

"My dearest friend, we are here beneath Teamhair, hot water and fresh clothes are waiting there. Come, rise and ready yourself as our quest is almost over."

Lulach looked up and smiled. "You have the same smooth tongue of your aunt."

With the mood a little more optimistic the group gathered up their belongings and set off towards the large shape looming through the morning mist.

As the four made their way up the hill towards the large wooden gate their spirits were lighter knowing that the High King would be generous in his hospitality, for it is the custom of the Gaels to make a stranger a guest under your roof.

As they approached the gate Niamh moved ahead and spoke to the guards. The guard leader looked over at the other three, and spending a little too much time looking and smiling at

Mordag, for the Danann was a handsome figure of a woman. Mordag not wishing to offend the guard smiled back.

"Drostan, hold my hand," she whispered.

Drostan immediately grabbed her hand and the disappointed and discouraged guard waved them through, giving them entry through the gate into the outer courtyard.

From a window high up Mòr looked down as the little group disappeared into the outer courtyard area, and started to scheme how she should foil whatever this little group are up to, for although no one had said what was happening, Mòr was more than just the person she professed to be and she could feel it in her bones, that something was afoot with these people.

"Two Danann's, a tatty looking Druid and a Priestess coming to Teamhair together and at this time. There's something going on and I'm going to find out what it is," she spat, with her hand tightly gripping the handle of the scian dubh that hung from her belt.

With that she quickly ran from the room and descended the stairs in the direction of the main hall.

Pushing past the guard she entered the room like a whirlwind. The door banged loudly as it hit a large brass door stopper fixed to the wall.

People stopped what they were doing and turned in the direction of the commotion.

Quickly four guards stepped in between the onrushing Mòr and the King stopping her in her tracks.

"I'm not here to harm the King," she shouted out. "I'm here to save him you fool's."

King Conn never moved but watched Mòr carefully.

"Remove your blade before you approach," bade the King, in a very calm manner.

Mòr stood there as the guard approached and removed her weapon.

"My lord," she laughed nervously. "I, I forgot it was there, a simple mistake," she said as she bowed.

"What do you want," questioned the King, somewhat disturbed by the intrusion.

Mòr looked up.

"There are four assassins in the Castle and I have come to warn the King to dispose of them before they can harm you."

Mòr spoke in a condescending tone.

There was a long silence as the High King surveyed the grand hall.

"And where are these dangerous assassins."

Mòr was becoming more agitated in her movements.

"They entered Teamhair less than one hour ago, in my opinion it would be better to find them and kill them before they can do their deed," she responded.

As the conversation was going on, one of the Kings Guard shut the heavy wooden entrance door and locked it.

Mòr suddenly felt trapped and very nervous.

"Tell me 'Druid', how do you know these things and why should I believe you," the King stared into her eyes.

"I captured one of the gang in the forest and tortured her until she confessed to me what their plans are. She told me that they hope to gain an audience with you and one of them who will be hiding a concealed weapon will suddenly leap forward and kill you," she proudly stated. "I swear to you it's true."

The King put his hand to his chin and tapped his lips with his first finger.

The Kings eyes darted towards a guard standing close by, and without saying another word the guard left the hall, quickly followed by two other guards.

Mòr was about to speak when the King put his finger to his lips.

"Hush, I don't wish to hear another word until the people you have accused are here with us, that is the way of the Gael."

The King sat back in his chair and patiently waited.

Although the room was fairly full you could have heard a pin drop on the floor. The people who were gathered there were like statues waiting on the High King to break the spell. Mòr looked around at the many faces, some looking at her and some looking away. In the corner was a person wrapped in a cloak and appeared to be sleeping.

"Gaels are stupid and drink too much," she thought, as she smiled nervously at the King.

The doors of the Great Hall burst open and the four travellers entered to the alarm and curiosity of all there. The guards brought them forward and stood them before the King. Mòr moved to one side and each looked the other in the eye.

Niamh was about to speak when the King asked politely whether or not they had eaten, as hospitality was important to the Gael.

The Priestess was a little taken back by this and went on to explain that they had eaten a few honey cakes and freshened up in the outer courtyard before entering the High Kings residence.

Mòr made a few grunting noises as she looked down her nose at the well travelled figures next to her.

Conn pretended not to notice Mòr's scorn and continued to speak.

"Who are you and what is your business here at Teamhair?"

Each in turn stepped forward and offered their names and then stepped back in line.

"Who will speak for you?" asked the King.

Niamh drew herself up to her full height and said, "My lord King Conn of Éirinn, my Danann friend has travelled far to bring you a message of the utmost importance."

With that the King waved Drostan forward. He reached into his vest and as he did so a guard stepped forward and he removed his hand so that the guard could retrieve what was there. Drostan stood with his arms open wide as the guard removed a scrolled document, which he promptly handed to the King.

106

Mòr moved forward to get a closer look but was waved back by the nearest guard.

The writing was of the ancient languages of the land and written in four columns. The first column was Fomorian. The second Fir Bholg. The third was Danann. And the fourth, the language of the Gael. All the columns were written in the Danann alphabet but phonetically in the tongue of each of the other languages.

The King scrutinised the scroll and then looked up.

Looking at Drostan he asked, "Do you know what this scroll reads?"

"Yes," replied Drostan.

"Do you understand what it says?"

"Yes."

"Can you read it to me here Drostan?" inquired the King.

"No," boomed a voice from the back of the hall. Within the blink of an eye, the Kings champion positioned himself, sword in hand, between the stranger and his lord.

The figure that was previously slumped apparently asleep at the back of the hall was now standing upright.

"What is written on that scroll is not for the ears of all men, it is a message for you great King."

"Identify yourself stranger and remove your hood," ordered the King.

"Not until you clear the great hall ... my identity is not for the likes of all here present." The Stranger spoke powerfully and with great authority.

By now the Kings guards had surrounded the stranger and had drawn their weapons.

"Remove your hood," demanded the King.

"I cannot do that Lord Conn, High King of Éirinn," repeated the stranger. "But I will remove it if you clear the great hall."

Conn could see that this was no time for a showdown, and he knew that the stranger was aware that it would be easy for the

King to have his hood removed by force if he so wished.

"Clear the hall," demanded the King. "Only my personal guard and the five strangers will stay."

"Accepted," said the tall cloaked figure.

Within the time it takes to draw your breath, the hall was emptied and the heavy oaken doors were closed with a dull thud, and before the sound of the locking bolt had stopped reverberating around the almost empty hall, the figure threw back his hood.

Lulach, who had been standing transfixed suddenly, let out a cry.

"Cathal," he gasped. "That's impossible. Your dead, I was at your burial … I saw you go into the ground. Is it really you?"

Cathal raised his arms slowly allowing his sleeves to fall back. There on the inside of his forearms were the unmistakable tattoos that marked this man as a Druid of the silver branch.

The King's champion moved forward to check for concealed weapons but the King waved him back in line with the swish of his arm.

"That will not be necessary," said the King. "But, answer the question that the Druid Lulach put to you," he demanded.

After a long and uncomfortable pause Cathal began to speak. This of course, for those of you who know about such things, is an old Druid trick to focus everyone's attention on what was about to be said, and with baited breathe all eyes were trained on the Druid.

"King Conn, fellow Druid, Danann friends," he began. "Priestess of Brighde, company of Gaels, there was a time when Éirinn averted disaster because of the sensibilities of our different tribes. The law stretched over the land and protected rich and poor, great and small, powerful and weak and our Druids were the keepers of that law.

From the days of the Solstice Corn Dollies till now Éirinn has been a peaceful land, but a shadow is looming bringing death and destruction in its wake."

The King shifted uneasily in his seat.

Cathal continued, "The Fomorian Francach, after his defeat of the 'Corn Dollies and Sun Wheels', fled back to the sea of Alba, badly wounded but not defeated, rested and recovered where his black heart continued to fester with hatred, and he immediately set about scheming how to wreak his revenge on those who foiled his plan all those years ago. He wormed his way into the court of the Fomorian King through cunning and sorcery, and set about casting his evil shadow, deceiving the King and the high lords with lies and deception."

"These are grave words indeed;" interrupted King Conn. "But what has this to do with us."

Cathal raised his hands and a light appeared like ball between them.

Everyone stood in awe, even the King sprang to his feet.

The light got brighter, and then from the middle of the ball a small black hole appeared and started to increase in size. After a moment or two, the black hole began to form pictures like a Scrying bowl.

The King moved forward to obtain a better view waving the soldiers away. The guards backed off except for the King's champion who still had his hand on the hilt of his sword in readiness of the unexpected. The King stared into the void and let out a long sigh for he could see sadness, turmoil and unrest. After a moment or two, Cathal spoke quietly.

"Tell us King Conn, what do you see?"

There was a long and baited silence before the King answered.

"Druid, I see anger and hatred and a large army that I cannot number preparing for war."

The King turned to face the Druid but before he could speak Cathal began to explain.

"In the days of your father King Fionntan." The Druid began. "Éirinn became sick because of the wicked schemes of a Fomorian named Francach. To cut a rather long and well known story short, and after a long and thorough search throughout the land, Francach, his plans foiled by the goodness of a young girl fled out of sight ... until now. Francach returned to his people and over the years he has beguiled his King and manipulated his people into breaking the ancient treaty that has stood between our peoples and his for millennia."

"Nobody has seen a Fomorian for over twenty-five years, how do we know that all of what you are saying is true?" enquired the King.

Mòr, seizing the moment of doubt pushed forward.

"Lies, lies and more lies King Conn," shrieked Mòr. "They are trying to deceive you, to bring you down so that the arrogant Danann's can usurp Éirinn again. Everyone knows they consider themselves superior to the Gaels."

King Conn ignored Mòr's outburst and continued.

"Convince me Druid of who you are and on who's authority do you speak and no tricks mind you."

Cathal raised an eyebrow that didn't go unnoticed.

"My Lord King, as you have heard by my old friend Lulach, you are looking at a dead man."

Most of those present were visibly shaken by those words, especially the guards who took a healthy step backwards.

Cathal continued, "After my passing my soul travelled west to where our ancestors are, in the land of Tír-nan-Og, there I was healed of all physical pains and as time moves much differently there, I recovered the vigour of my young manhood. I spent much time resting and learning from my forefathers about the things that really matter, things that are so difficult to grasp in a mortal lifetime."

On hearing this, the King dropped back into his seat, and the rest of the company, including Mòr, looked on in absolute wonder.

"It came to the attention of the Goddess that war is being prepared beneath the waves in the sea of Alba and that Éirinn would be overrun and darkness would cover the land again. Éirinn is a sacred land and although that in times to come she would sleep under the oversight of another power, a greater power, Éirinn will remain a special place for Gods and men alike."

Cathal gave out a long breathe and his image became like gossamer.

"My strength is fading for it is not easy for one to transport one's image from the blessed isles into the realms of the living."

Cathal's image was all but gone when the King stepped forward and moved his hand through the disappearing Druid. The King's champion, fearing trickery took the Kings arm and gently moved it away.

The King stood silent for a moment collecting his thoughts.

"Did everyone see what I just saw?"

Each nodded in turn as the Kings enquiring eyes fell upon them.

"As a boy my father spoke often of Cathal the Druid," spoke the King. "He had great affection for him and trusted Cathal with his life and land. I have no doubt that Cathal appeared in my court to substantiate the validity of your story Drostan.

The point is, is what are we going to do about this threat without bringing war to the land?"

Mòr stepped forward.

"My lord King, you are being deceived by these people and the image of the Druid was nothing more than an illusion. If you raise your army and march to the north-eastern shores of Ulster, it will appear as a threat and that you are the one who is breaking the time honoured treaty."

Everyone looked to the King for a decision. Drostan had the scroll from the Danann council. The young Priestess Niamh was obviously sincere and honest. Lulach was sure that the apparition was indeed Cathal speaking from the 'otherworld', and Mòr, Mòr was tricky, but her words were well chosen, and yes, if the King were to gather an army it could be seen as an aggressive act and could begin a war that none wanted.

"I will gather with my councillors and we will discuss what must be done. Accommodation and food will be prepared for you; stay in your rooms until we are ready to speak further ... that is an order from the High King of Éirinn. Is that understood?"

The guards unlocked the great oaken doors and the King and his troop disappeared at a pace down the long corridor.

"This way then," ordered the guard, and the company of Gael, Danann and Mòr, for nobody was sure who she was, followed the guard up several flights of stairs to rooms prepared for guests.

Niamh and the Crows

Seán and Ban Dubh

Mòr insisted that she had a room to herself, and the others agreed without resistance for no one wished to share a room with Mòr who was proving to be as slippery as an eel. The others agreed that Niamh and Mordag should share the cosy room, with Drostan and Lulach in the more basic area. After the four friends had put their belongings in their respective rooms, the two men went and joined the women in the cosy room. The fire burned bright and with the sweet smell of peat filling the air, the warmth could be felt regardless of where one sat.

They all sat silent as they mulled over their thoughts.

Suddenly Niamh sat bolt upright.

"Can you hear Mòr talking?" she addressed the Danann's, for the Danann's have very acute hearing.

"Yes, I can hear her talking with someone," chipped in Mordag.

"I thought she was on her own," whispered Lulach.

"She is," answered Niamh, as she sprang to her feet heading for the door.

"What are you doing Niamh?" enquired the Danann woman.

Niamh moved away from the others and placing her hand over her broach, glanced back, and whispered something the others couldn't make out, and she instantly transformed into a cockroach. Scurrying under the door and out into the hallway she made her way quickly down the hall to the next door and slipped silently under the gap and into the room. Once there she found a safe place to conceal herself and watched Mòr as she talked into what appeared to be a wooden box with holes in the sides.

Niamh thought she could hear something scratching in the box, but was too far away to get a good view.

"Tell my brother that the seeds of doubt and suspicion have been planted in the mind of that old fool King Conn. Tell him that the King is twixt the hammer and the anvil. He thinks that if he raises an army he will be seen as the perpetrator of aggression and a war monger."

Mòr gave out a stifled laugh.

"By the time he plucks up enough courage his Kingdom will be ours again ... as it should be. Act quickly brother, prepare the army and strike while Éirinn is weak."

Again Mòr gave out a cackle and suddenly, without warning turned quickly as if she was aware that someone or something was in the room listening.

Her eyes scanned the shadows watching for any unexpected movement.

Niamh, in the form of an insect stayed perfectly still.

Mòr gave out a long breath and cursed in an undertone, and turning back to the box and addressed whatever was in it.

"Take this message to Francach, let's set this plan into motion."

With that she lifted the box off the table and moved towards the window. The wooden window shutter was locked and she couldn't open it.

"Damn these wretched Gaels." Mòr spat as she looked around for something to force the window open.

Niamh scurried silently around the walls until she reached the wall beneath the window. Looking around for where Mòr was, for Mòr was preoccupied searching for something, anything that could be used to get the window open. Niamh effortlessly climbed the wall and up onto the window ledge. Again she turned to see where Mòr was. Mòr was over the other side of the room rummaging through an old oak chest, cursing and swearing at her lack of success in finding what she required. Niamh moved closer to the box when suddenly a pointed dark beak thrust out and nearly caught her unawares. The insect moved back out of range. Again Niamh looked across the room at Mòr who was continuing her frantic search. Quickly the insect ran down the wall and behind a large chair, and momentarily appeared as Niamh the human before transforming into a large crow. Mòr turned around as if she had heard something, looked at the box on the sill where she had left it and continued her search. Niamh the crow leapt up onto the windowsill and approached the box.

"Who are you?" asked Niamh quietly in the tongue of crows. There was a long silence before the crow inside the box replied.

"My name is Ban-Dubh and the servant of Mòr."

With one eye watching Mòr, Niamh continued the conversation with Ban-Dubh.

"A servant of Mòr?" enquired Niamh.

"Not a willing servant" continued Ban-dubh. "Mòr told me that when Éirinn is returned to the Fomorians, Francach will exterminate every bird of the crow family in the land".

"Ban-Dubh" whispered Niamh, "when Mòr releases you to deliver your message to Francach, go back to your people and await my call. Under no circumstances go to Francach for he will without fail kill you after you have delivered Mòr's message."

Niamh continued, "Good King Conn and all that is good in Éirinn, under and above, are planning to thwart Mòr and Francach and their evil plans, do this and you and your people will be safe."

Ban-Dubh first hesitated and then nodded in agreement and Niamh silently floated down again behind the chair. A moment later she appeared as a cockroach again running around the skirting and back to safety under the heavy furniture and importantly out of the reach of Mòr.

Not finding anything useful in the chest, Mòr slammed the lid down only to discover a heavy metal key protruding out of the lock.

"Good, good she shrieked, this will have to do."

Mòr went to the window and jamming the key under the latch and with more than a little effort, the latch pin that was holding the window shut snapped and the window shutter swung open.

"Ah, now we can proceed with our plan," said Mòr excitedly. She opened the box and roughly took out the crow.

"Now do as I asked and we will all get what we deserve," threatened Mòr.

She opened her hand and the bird flew out into the chilly evening air. Mòr watched as the bird circled getting its bearings; suddenly the crow turned south and was gone.

"Damn that idiot bird," cried Mòr, and with that she threw the box out of the window and listened as it smashed as it hit the hard ground below. "I'll deal with you and your kin later," she spat.

With that Mòr slammed the window shutter shut, and spun around walking quickly towards the warmth of the fire, and there she settled down in a large comfortable chair muttering under her breath and with the occasional stamp of her angry foot.

Meanwhile in the other room, Niamh was quickly explaining to the others what she had just seen and heard.

Mordag, still remembering the nasty bump to her head inflicted by Mòr suggested that it might be for the best if they disposed of Mòr now, rather than later.

The others chuckled at the idea but knew that Mordag was probably speaking tongue in cheek.

"Who is this Ban-Dubh you speak of Niamh?" questioned Lulach.

"We didn't have much time to exchange pleasantries, but from what I understand she is the queen of crows and was trapped by one of Mòr's servants during her travels through the land and seconded under threat into Mòr's service."

"Okay, what do we do now" whistled Mordag as she paced the floor.

"Perhaps if you stood still for a moment we could try to work out our next move". Mordag reacted with a very tired scowl. The words came from Drostan who up until now had remained quiet. "I think we should talk with the King and see if he has any suggestions."

One after the other they all nodded their heads in agreement. "But first let's get some sleep and refresh ourselves from our long journey."

"Very sensible" muttered Lulach, and with that they all retired to their beds and no more was spoken.

The morning broke with the usual birdsong, but the sky was overcast throwing a greyish hue into the room through narrow slits in the shutter. Sounds of activity could be heard from the castle staff and whispered voices as people passed by the door as servants made their way down the corridor. One by one the group of four stirred from sleep. Looking towards the window there was no way of guessing what period of time of the day it was because the sun could not be seen traversing the sky. Suddenly and without warning there was a fluttering and scratching at the shutter. Mordag was about to throw a boot at the window when Niamh jumped up and ran to open the shuttered window. The window was of course locked with a pin.

"Can somebody help me get this pin out of the window" she called. "Hurry, it's a friend."

Drostan was the first to react, and reaching down into his boot produced a slim short bladed knife that only the Danann's had the skill to produce. The others looked at him in surprise.

"Okay, so I omitted to tell the guards I had this in my boot." Drostan shrugged his shoulders and smiled a very broad mischievous smile.

Within a moment Drostan had the pin out of the window frame and the window shutter swung open.

Niamh took the silver horn in her hand and whispered the incantation that is written upon it. Instantly the language of the bird could be understood by all present.

"That's better," said the crow, with more than a touch of jollity.

"Ban-Dubh, what are you doing back here?" asked Niamh.

The crow hurriedly continued, "I told my people everything that you told me, and we are gathering all our brethren to readiness. The sea birds tell us that there is a lot of activity on the shoreline between Éirinn and Alba. If we are to avert a war we must act quickly. Speak with the King, tell him to send out riders to prove that what you are saying is true … do it now, there is no time to lose."

The group of four began to feverishly prepare themselves to meet the King.

"What will you do now?" questioned Niamh.

"My husband Seán-Dubh and I along with our clan will roost in the woods that surround Teamhair. We will be in readiness for your signal for you are not alone at this dark time."

With that the crow shot through the open window in the direction of the distant trees.

Niamh looked round at the others. Come, it's time to talk with the high King of Éirinn.

Two very large guards escorted the group to the main hall where the King already sat. To the side and below the Kings table sat Mòr, she was already eating and drinking. As the others came closer she stopped and looked suspiciously at what their intentions might be.

"Sit, and break your fast for I have a feeling that today may turn out to be very interesting" invited the King that sounded more like an order.

They sat down opposite Mòr who said nothing but curling her lip and digging her long dirty fingernails into the wooden table.

"The atmosphere is too tense" spoke the King, "send for a musician to lighten our gathering."

"No need" chirped Lulach "Just fetch me a Cláirseach and I will sing you a song, even at this unknowing hour."

The King waved his hand and a servant rushed out of the door, and within seconds reappeared with the very instrument in his hands. The servant placed it on the table next to Lulach the Druid who began to un-wrap the seal skins that protected the Cláirseach from the elements. As the wrappings fell from the instrument Lulach gasped at the sight before him.

"My harp, my old harp," cried Lulach with more than a tear and a quaver in his voice. Lulach placed his hand on the frame and a sound like a sigh emitted from the instrument. The spirit that resides in every harp recognises its harpist and its common knowledge that each harp has its own individual personality. This harp was no different, and it was obvious that the Cláirseach was as pleased to be reunited with its harpist as the harpist was with his harp.

"Thank you my lord King" bowed Lulach.

The King smiled, "sing for us Druid" he said softly.

Lulach took a moment to tune his old friend and then he gently strummed across the strings. The notes floated high into the ceiling and seemed to dance along the oaken beams that supported this most magnificent hall. Within minutes the whole space was filled with the most beautiful sounds, so beautiful in fact that even the most hardened warrior had a tear in his eye as each note conjured sweet memories of home. Guards could be heard whispering the names of wives, sweethearts and children as they were swept along on this most magical and melancholy wave. Sadness and laughter intertwined with each exquisite note and then Lulach began to sing. He sang of Éirinn of old when Danann, Fomorian and Gael fought battles for supremacy, finishing with how peace was reached with honour and dignity. Hearts and spirits were raised by the wonder of the song, even Mòr, at least for a brief moment, seemed to soften. But sadly it was short lived.

As soon as the sound had died away Mòr stood up and began to accuse the Druid of trickery.

"Silence" ordered the King.

Mòr sat down again, muttering under her breath.

The room fell into silence for what seemed an age, and then the King spoke again.

"I have seen some marvellous things in my time as high King, but what is happening now and the things that we have all witnessed are almost unbelievable. I want everyone to clear the hall except my most trusted guards and the young Priestess known as Niamh."

Mòr sprang to her feet and was just about to complain when the King's champion placed a heavy hand on her shoulder forcing her back down again. It also had the desired effect of silencing her wicked tongue. The King ignored the outburst and without raising his head, he signalled with a wave of his hand that the rest of the company should leave the room. Drostan, Mordag and Lulach left the hall swiftly, whereas Mòr moved slowly and threateningly, glancing over at the young Priestess with menace and hatred.

A guard pushed her forward and she shrugged in defiance at his touch. She left the room after making a sigil of ill fortune, and sneered as the door closed behind her.

Niamh made the sign of a counter spell, and the King who was watching with interest, smiled at the brave Priestess with approval.

"Come closer" ordered the King.

Niamh moved closer until the King's champion crossed his spear across Niamh's path.

"No need for that" said the King.

The champion stood back.

"Tell me Niamh, do you believe what the Danann's have told us?"

Niamh looked up at the King and answered, "My lord King Conn, I am convinced beyond all doubt that the threat from the Fomorian is real. Why they have chosen to take such action is a mystery, but if and when we respond to the threat and make our way to the coast I have a way of uncovering who is behind this."

The King looked Niamh in the eye. "Priestess, there is a lot at stake here; the future of Éirinn is at risk. Convince me now that what you say is true and show me the evidence that I need to march an army into a dreadful war."

Niamh thought for a moment and then asked if the King would allow her to bring her special things into the great hall.

A servant and two guards were immediately dispatched and within a few minutes the door burst back open with the servant carrying Niamh's cloak containing her magical tools. The King looked curiously on as Niamh attached the silver horn on her belt. Then she clipped the Broach of Danu securely on her shawl, and finally she held her rainbow staff and stood before the King.

King Conn raised himself from his chair to better observe the fine items that Niamh had in her possession.

"Alright" said the King, "what happens now?"

Niamh took on the authority of a Priestess of Brighde and whispered something under her breath and raised the silver horn to her lips and blew a long resonating note.

The King and all those present placed their hands over their ears as the sound reverberated off the thick stone walls of the hall.

Within seconds, two black crows appeared at the open

window and hopped inside and coming to rest perching on the back of a nearby chair. One of the guards moved forward.

"No" yelled the Priestess, "they are friends."

The guard returned to his position but watched the two birds seemingly without blinking, as only a guard can.

"My lord King," continued Niamh turning to the King. "Allow me to introduce King Seán-Dubh and his queen Ban-Dubh."

The King was perplexed.

Ban-Dubh spoke up. "King Conn of the Gaels, we have news of a great army gathering off the shore of the Sea of Alba that will bring death and destruction to your land, and in the broader sense, our land."

The King staggered back on hearing the crow speak.

"What trickery is this," called the King, directing his words towards the Priestess.

"These gifts were given to me by the lord of the forest, who some call 'the green man' as an aid in bringing peace to our land.

The King was stunned into silence for a brief moment as the thoughts of what he was witnessing hit home like an arrow shot from a bow. Then, without warning he jumped to his feet and whispered to his personal guard to dispatch three of his best riders on the fastest horses in Teamhair to the coast. His instructions were clear, observe anything unusual and report back as quickly as possible.

Seán-Dubh interrupted, "My lord King, some of my birds will escort your riders creating a safe passage for them."

The high King although still in a state of shock nodded his approval.

The crow continued, "Some of the sea birds have been telling us that a powerful Fomorian named Francach and his sister are the perpetrators of this impending war. By what we have learned, the woman Mòr who is here in this castle is the sister. The owls in the south say that she murdered a Druid who was on his way to deliver advice from the Druid High Council, and after disposing of his body she used his mission to get to you. If she cannot physically stop you she will attempt to mislead the high King and therefore thwart any plans you make by lies, the dark side, and cunning." The bird persisted, "She has travelled the land gathering information as to the where abouts the magical gifts of the Danann's are. We know that she has discovered that the Cauldron of Plenty is right here in Teamhair."

"How" enquired the King.

"The house sparrows that nest within these walls told us that she used her incantations to extract information from some of your most trusted servants, and after she had what she wanted, she wiped their memories clean. She is indeed a dangerous woman."

"Do we have any proof that this woman is a spy and a murderer" asked the King, now worried that his security had been breached.

The crow continued, "She has a bag with evidence of her guilt inside it. Look in the bag and you will see that we are telling you the truth."

"Fetch Mòr and her bag, and don't give her reason to suspect that we are on to her little scheme" instructed the King to his guards.

The guards left the hall, but before the ringing of the great oaken doors had subsided the guards rushed back in.

"She's gone," panted the first guard. "She must have overheard the conversation in this room, and she's took her bag and left."

"Find her," called the King.

But before any of his guards could respond Ban-Dubh spoke up.

"I think we can now assume that Mòr is guilty?"

The King nodded in agreement.

"We will deal with Mòr and you deal with her brother," called Seán-Dubh, and the two birds flew out of the window and into the open sky.

The King turned to his champion and instructed him to prepare the men for war, and then he turned to Niamh.

"Niamh, we have a several hours before my riders return, sit with me and tell me about how all of this started."

Niamh started to unfold her story beginning in the village of the salmon, and the finding of Drostan in the sea. She told him in great detail about receiving the gifts of the Goddess Danu, and the journey through the forest and the bazaar meeting with the 'Green Man' and the unfortunate encounter with Mòr in the forest. The injury and capture of Mordag, the journey ending here in Teamhair and standing before the High King of Éirinn.

While Niamh told her tale, the King had shifted uneasily in his chair watching a candle burning down the hours. The candle burned slowly and the occasion drop of molten wax would run down the side cooling and setting on its journey creating weird patens on the base of the candle holder.

A loud noise from outside jerked the King back to the present as the sound of horse hoofs clattered on the stony ground of the courtyard below.

"They're back," declared the King's champion.

The King sprang to his feet and stood looking at the large hall door in expectation of his riders. The King didn't have to wait long, the doors burst open and three exhausted men entered the room panting.

There was a short silence as the King observed each man in turn.

"Well!" questioned the King. "Is there anything unusual to report from the coast?"

The first rider started to affirm the Kings fears by reporting that a large number of physically distorted giants were bringing supplies out of the sea and loading them up on the beach. The second rider spoke of war machines being assembled in readiness, and the third rider also confirmed that further to the south a large encampment had been erected for a large army.

The King sat slowly down again, calling his most trusted advisors to his side.

"Ideally," declared the King, "It would be better for us if we could contain the Fomorians on the beach, but time is against us, we must gather and ready the men from all the provinces. It may take days and the men from the south will be tired from their journey. Any suggestions?" asked the King hopefully.

"I can give you time," said the young Priestess.

The men swung around to look at the diminutive figure of the Priestess standing before them.

"How?" asked the King.

Niamh continued, "The Fomorians have lived in the sea since the great battles of old. They are not acclimatised to the land or the warmth of the sun. That is why they have chosen to invade our shores in winter when the weather in wet and cold, almost perfect conditions for a Fomorian, wouldn't you say?"

"The girl is right" called out one of the advisors. "But how do we hold them were they are until the warmer weather comes?

The King's personal guard murmured amongst themselves declaring the notion as foolish and irrelevant.

"Wait," spoke up the King. "Niamh, what do have you in mind? We in this great hall have seen some wondrous things this day and you Niamh have been at the centre if everything. We need three days to collect the men and ready them for the fight. Can you give us three days?"

Niamh drew herself up to her full height, which wasn't very high at the best of times, but holding her staff aloft she called aloud an incantation that no other than mortal could understand.

Suddenly, there was a sound like a crack of thunder that shook the very foundations of Teamhair. The guards and the councillors all looked on in absolute dread and amazement. King Conn held on to his chair for fear of falling over, for what seemed like an earth quake had struck Éirinn.

"Quickly, open the doors," yelled the King, and they all rushed forward as the large oaken doors swung back. "To the battlements," called the King at the top of his voice. They rushed up the stairs meeting Drostan, Mordag and Lulach on the way.

"What's happening?" asked Drostan totally confused at seeing this group of people rushing frantically up the stairs. "It's normal behaviour to leave the building rather than go to the top of it in these cases, not that it happens very often."

His words were ignored as the group ran passed him.

"Come on," insisted Mordag, "I'm not sure what's happening myself, but I'm sure it's important." The three friends hurriedly followed the others to the top of the stairs and ran to join them as the group observed the sky in the north east.

The group gathered at the eastern battlement and peered over at the angry sky. None of them had ever seen a sky like this one. Although it was fairly dark, the heavens over the eastern lands were like a pot of boiling black bubbling tar. Within the swirling mass flashes of lightening could be seen, turning the fuming, churning blackness into a terrifying scene.

Niamh stood transfixed at the awesome power that she had unleashed. Her face had drained of any colour, and she looked like a ghost in the darkness.

"What have you done girl?" called Conn.

Everyone turned to face the young Priestess, though she said nothing.

Suddenly, her face began to glow, brighter and brighter until her whole being was like a shining star in the heavens. Her arms moved outwards and her feet lifted from the ground. She floated before them for a second or two, and then she spoke.

As if given a silent command all those present dropped to

their knees and covered their faces, even the King was on his knees.

"Men of Éirinn," she boomed. "Do not be afraid, for what you are seeing is your deliverance, not your end. I am the Goddess Danu and I have come to aid you at this most difficult time. The Fomorian folk are not your enemy; they have been misled by a man named Francach and his sister Mòr. He escaped beneath the waves many years ago after plotting to overthrow Éirinn in the days of your fathers. Even now after all this time, his hatred of the Gael and the Danann has not diminished, in fact, it is more poisonous and twisted than ever."

Conn peeped through his fingers at the shining figure before him, thinking that he would probably wake up shortly for this must surely be a terrifying dream.

"You dare to look upon the face of your Goddess, Conn? Then you have your father's bravery within you and if you put your trust in this my Priestess, you will without doubt prevail as King, and Éirinn will flourish forever as the emerald isle she surely is. King Conn of the Gaels, I Danu queen of the ancient ones say this, your name will be forever remembered as the King who brought wisdom to the land, bringing everlasting peace to the peoples who populate Éirinn, now and in the future, above the land and under the land, beyond the sea and under the sea."

With that there was a long silence as each person present looked up at the star-like shining figure of Niamh as she hung silently above the battlements. One by one they rose to their feet and walked around the suspended figure of the Priestess.

Drostan was the first to speak. "Does anyone here have any doubts that this young girl is the instrument of the Goddess?"

There was a lot of shaking of heads and a few mumbled no's as they each looked on transfixed by the wondrous sight before them.

Then slowly the bright light began to fade and the young

Priestess floated gently down to the ground.

Mordag was the first to react as she raced forward and supported Niamh as her legs gave way under her. The King placed his cloak on the floor and Mordag lay the girl down as all eyes observed the Priestess at the centre of this amazing event.

"Quickly," ordered the King. "Bring her some water ... no! Make that wine."

With that one of the guards raced off down the stairs.

The King glanced back over his shoulder at the raging sky in the east and said, "What now my friends? I think we may have a busy time ahead of us," and with those words still ringing in everyone's ears there was a rush of warm air that engulfed Teamhair.

"It's begun," declared the King.

The Road to the Sea of Alba

The group made their way down the stairs with the King ordering preparations as they went. The Danann's followed behind supporting Niamh who looked like she needed a rest to recover from her most unusual experience. The King and his advisor's continued down the stairs as Drostan, Mordag, Lulach and Niamh peeled away in the direction of their rooms. Once in the room they lay poor Niamh on her couch and left her to sleep.

"Come, let's go down to the main hall and join the King. We can leave Niamh here to sleep and fill her in later with what has been decided," whispered Mordag.

Lulach looked back at the young Priestess as the three companions left the room and smiled.

"She is so young to carry such a burden," he thought to himself.

He quietly closed the door and they made their way along the corridor and down the winding stone stairs toward the Great Hall.

Niamh slept soundly; unaware that she was not alone, for unseen behind the heavy wall drapes stood the figure of Mòr. The warm air was now permeating the castle and Mòr was beginning to perspire, for Fomorians do not like the heat.

Before he left, Lulach had opened the window shutters but the breeze coming into the room was warm and sticky, and Mòr was beginning to feel very uncomfortable in her heavy robes.

On the window ledge stood a house sparrow observing what was happening in the room. Quickly, as only house sparrows can, he darted off in the direction of the trees that make up the beginning of the wood to the south of Teamhair.

Mòr roughly loosened her collar as the heat and her nerves tingled with expectation of what she had in mind. Her hand drifted slowly down to the small dagger that was sheathed hanging from her belt. She griped the handle with a sweaty palm and lifted the glistening blade upwards. A cruel smile broke across her face. Being careful not to wake the sleeping Priestess she carefully drew back the drapes and entered the room with great stealth. The sweat ran down her face as she crossed the room towards the couch. She could feel her pulse beating in her ears as the excitement of the moment filled her with power. Her heart pounded in her breast and she had to check herself for fear of moving too quickly and spoiling the moment. She turned her attention to the door and listened for sounds of anyone outside, but it was conveniently quiet. The moment had come for Mòr to silence this troublesome Priestess once and for all. She held the knife aloft and moved closer to the couch for she knew that opportunities like this don't come too often. Keeping her eye on the rise and fall of the priestess's breathing, she raised her hand high ready to plunge the dagger through Niamh's heart. Relishing the moment she laughed inwardly at just how easy this was going to be.

"Just one more step and it is done" she thought.

No sooner had her foot taken that extra step then a terrible pain shot through her arm. The pain was so intense that she cried out, and dropping the dagger she looking up at her arm and saw her own blood running down it. There was a large open gash on the back of her hand. She looked at the sleeping Priestess who fortunately for her lay undisturbed. She glanced around the room for the perpetrator of her injury, but could see no one. She reached down to retrieve the knife, this time with much more caution. Her eyes were flickering from side to side as she raised herself up again to fulfil her foul intention. Sweat was again pouring down her face and into her eyes as she fought to regain her composure. Bang! She was hit in the face by something very fast and very hard, and she fell backwards over a small stool landing heavily on the stone floor. There was blood on her face and she raised her hand to wipe it off. Suddenly she felt the pain and by the feel of her fingertips she became aware that her right eye ball was missing. Fear and trembling struck her at the thought that something in this room was protecting the Priestess, an evil spirit perhaps? With one hand covering her missing eye she glanced across the room in the direction of the sleeping Priestess only to see her sitting up rubbing her eyes from sleep. Mòr scrambled to her feet and grabbing the dagger that still lay on the stone floor. She made her way unsteadily towards the astonished Priestess who could now see Mòr with blood on her face and a knife in her hand. With her right arm raised to strike and her left hand protecting her face, she towered over the terrified Priestess. Suddenly, from behind the priestess rushed a black flapping swarm stabbing and pecking with razor sharp beaks. Mòr dropped the knife in surprise and lashed out with her arms attempting to ward off the black storm that was forcing her backwards. Step by step she was forced back away from Niamh. The dark fury was unrelenting in its ferocity and Mòr was driven further back towards the open window. The air coming in was hot and choking and Mòr was yelping like a pup that had been scolded by its mother. There were feathers everywhere and the eerie squawking so loud it could have raised the dead.

The King's guards obviously disturbed by the racket that could be heard all over the castle burst into the room, just in time to see Mòr falling backwards out of the open window with a loud scream. One of the guards rushed to the window while the other cradled Niamh in his arms, she was obviously shaken by Mòr's murderous objective.

The guard at the window looked down at the broken body of Mòr lying below.

"Well, she's dead now," said the guard, with more than a degree of satisfaction in his voice. "She really was a nasty piece of work that one," he said, shaking his head.

His colleague nodded in agreement.

"Are you alright miss?" enquired the guard at the window.

"Yes, I'm fine, thanks to my friends here" answered the Priestess, her arm raised and motioning around the room.

The two guards looked around the room at the multitude of birds sitting on the furniture.

"Well, bless the Goddess, that's all I can say," chirped the guard. "I've never seen anything like it; in fact, there are a lot of things happening at the moment that I don't understand."

Niamh smiled "We're not finished yet."

As her words tapered off, the King and the others exploded into the room.

"What in the name of the Dagdha has been going on in here?" called out the King.

The guards explained very quickly, I might add, that Mòr, who everyone had thought had fled the castle, had in fact been hiding waiting for the opportunity to murder the young Priestess Niamh, and that these birds had attacked Mòr and forced her out of the window.

The King stood silent for a moment and then walked over to the window. Looking down he saw a crumpled mass of clothing and almost every carrion bird for miles around feeding furiously off the carcass.

"Are you absolutely sure it was Mòr?" asked the King.

"Yes, my lord," confirmed the guards, and even Niamh reassured the King that the person who tried to murder her was indeed Mòr.

"Good," called out the King, "that's one less to worry about."

With that he turned about and made his way out of the room, quickly followed by his guards.

"You can deal with our friends can you not?" enquired the King in the direction of Drostan.

With that the King turned and bowed a majestic bow in the direction of the birds and then left.

Drostan, Mordag and Lulach had been standing at the door, now came in.

"We had no idea that Mòr was in the room Niamh," apologized Mordag solemnly.

The others nodded in agreement.

"You had no way of knowing," said Niamh, "Mòr was indeed a slippery character and besides, we all thought she had slipped away from Teamhair while we were in the Great Hall convincing the King of Éirinn's danger."

Niamh stood up and called out the name of Ban-Dubh. One of the large black crows squawked loudly.

"Sorry" called Niamh reaching for her silver horn.

A quick blast on the horn and a few well chosen magical words and once more humans and birds were able to share each other's speech.

Ban-Dubh spoke up. "Niamh ... Priestess of the Goddess, I thank you for setting me free and for removing the awful threat to my people that was Mòr the Fomorian. With the help of my brothers and sisters and a very nosy little house sparrow, we have saved your life and brought this evil woman down. My people and our cousins have disposed of her body and her bones will be taken by the owls to the wolves who reside in the mountains to sharpen their pup's teeth upon. You can keep her clothes if you wish as we have no need of extra covering, our feathers are just fine. We are flying back to our nests now, but we will see you soon for we will not desert you."

With that the birds flew out of the open window and into the muggy sky.

The preparations went well over the next couple of days. Large groups of fighting men of the Gaels arrived in intervals. Many of them looked exhausted with the heat, and they were met with refreshments by the Kings own men. Men from each province gathered in large groups while the Kings servants served great quantities of food and water in a never ending supply. The High King was back in the great hall with the Kings and commanders of the biggest army the Gaels had ever mustered since the legendary wars against the Danann's many years ago, so long ago, in fact, no one living could remember them but were kept fresh in the memory by bardic tales and songs.

Within hours of eating, drinking and resting the tired men were fully recharged with energy and were eager to meet the unknown enemy for the provincial Kings had been told not to tell the men about whom or what they would be facing. Gaels are by nature brave, but they are also superstitious and it would have been risky giving the soldiers information that they may misunderstand, spreading false and frightening stories amongst themselves and demoralizing the men just before battle. The only thing the men had been told is that the unseasonal weather was due to the God Lugh visiting the halls of Brugh Na Bóinne and was seen as a blessing on the land. This appeared to pacify everyone, and spirits were high, at least for the time being.

The birds kept flying in with information about the Fomorian movements and Niamh passed it on to the High King. The news was indeed good as the hot weather was keeping the Fomorians under the sea, giving the Gaels precious time to prepare.

The High King and his commanders worked out a battle plan and decided that the plan be filtered down through those in charge and the clan chiefs. This was agreed and that in two days hence, the army of the Gaels would march to meet the mostly unknown and ancient enemy.

Niamh sat in the room alone as the others had gone off to find out what the Kings intentions were.

"Niamh, Niamh," called a voice quietly from the lengthening shadows on the other side of the room.

Niamh, still unnerved by recent events spun around expecting to see the impossible, that is, Mòr standing there with a knife in her hand.

Her fear soon turned to joy when she saw who it was.

"Oh, I am so glad to see you again, great Lord."

The Greenman smiled.

"And I you, young Priestess," groaned the Greenman. "Niamh, Our friend Fionntan the Salmon has been to the Sea of Alba, he has seen the frustration and confusion that is happening there. The Fomorian army is losing its patience with Francach saying he cannot deliver his promises. He is becoming more and more maddened by events and the heat created by the weather elements will not hold him back for ever. So far Francach has remained relatively safe under the sea, but soon he will venture out and he has a reckoning with the Great Goddess Danu. He escaped once because Danu thought he would have learned his lesson and humbled himself. Unfortunately for him and his black heart, he has learned nothing. Firstly he poisoned his sister's heart against the Gael, and secondly he turned the Fomorian people against the ancient covenant that their own forefathers had agreed upon, namely that the Fomorian would take the seas, the Gael would take the land above, and the Danann would occupy the realms beneath the lands, the invisible domain.

The Goddess has told me to tell you this, go to the King Niamh and tell him to march his army to the coast overlooking the Sea of Alba. Once there he must stretch his men along the edge of the shore line and wait. When the Fomorian emerge from the sea, fall back to the dunes and take up a defensive line."

The Greenman rustled his leaves and stepped back into the shadows, and before Niamh could utter a word he faded into nothing and was gone.

She moved to the window and looked out at the afternoon sun peeping through the swirling mists of heat that the elements had generated. Mopping the sweat from her brow, she prepared herself to inform the King of what the Greenman had told her. Within the blink of an eye, she was making her way along the corridor and down the stairs to the Great Hall where Conn and the other great men of the Gaels were gathered.

It was obvious by her reception that the High King had told the others about what had occurred over the last couple of days, and as Niamh entered the Hall a great show of reverence was given her. Men bowed low and Kings removed their golden crowns, symbols of office and power. Soldiers and guards raised their swords and spears in recognition of her special position as Priestess of the Goddess. In response, Niamh raised her arms high allowing her loose sleeves to fall back, exposing the entwining snakes tattooed on the inside of both forearms. At first as if in awe, there was a mighty hush, but then, spontaneously and quickly, followed by a hearty cheer, as all present showed their trust in this petite young woman. Even Conn High King of all Éirinn went down on one knee before the Priestess, and one by one all followed suit until everyone present, including her friends kneeled before her. Niamh stepped closer and lowered her arms. The Hall became silent with expectation and all eyes were fixed on the Priestess.

What happened next is legend. Stories and songs record the stirring speech she gave. Bards and poets, travelling storytellers and men around camp fires would recall her inspiring words down through the ages. Fathers would recite her words in prose to children for there were lessons to be learned about pride and justice, love and honour. This was not just a speech for the ears of a few, no! This was a rousing of a nation, words that made the chest puff out and the blood pump with dignity and self respect. The nation of Éirinn became one nation.

"People and friends of the Gael," she began. She recited all that the Greenman had told her, and then she reached into her pouch and retrieved something wondrous and opening her palm flat for all to see, there resting on her hand was a small golden acorn. Niamh took a breath and breathed gently on the small object resting on her hand. Instantly it began to sprout. There was a loud ooh sound from those watching.

"What does it mean?" enquired Conn.

"It means a covenant between the Gael, Danann, Fir Bholg, Fomorian and any other race that come as friends. It's a pact between the deities and us, and as long as Éirinn has peace the pact and the blessings will continue forever."

"But first," declared the Priestess, "we have a wrong to right."

The King sprung to his feet and drew his sword. Holding it aloft, he shouted, "Prepare the men, we leave at dawn."

With that the meeting closed as men rushed outside to pass on instructions to the soldiers gathered there. Naturally, it wasn't long before word got around about the inspirational speech and the wondrous happenings that had come from the young Priestess. The men were in high spirits, united in one purpose and perfectly ready to do their duty.

The morning came soon enough, hot and sticky, yet the optimism of the night before had not diminished. Battle hard soldiers greeted each other which was uncommon, in fact, unheard of during the prelude to war. The mood was one of confidence brought about by trust; trust in a small Priestess that had the favour of the Goddess.

The great army took formation outside of Teamhair with most of the mounted warriors taking the lead. They were followed by men on foot, marching with such vigour you would have thought they were marching to a banquet instead of a battle. At the back rode more mounted warriors and the Kings Druidic advisors. With this group were Lulach, Drostan and Mordag. The High King and the other Kings along with Niamh were up front, surrounded by their respective champions.

The long column had been on the road for less than two

hours when the sky turned black over their heads. The marching army stopped as the High King raised his arm. Many of the soldiers looked nervously skyward. Niamh pushed ahead until she was forward of the leading group. Niamh instinctively blew the magical silver horn as a great black bird swooped down.

"Niamh," cried the crow. "Our friends the sea birds inform us that there is renewed activity under the sea, you must make haste."

"Thank you Ban Dubh," said the Priestess.

"It's Seán Dubh actually, but that's okay, you all look the same to us too," squawked the crow with a twinkle in his eye. "Pass the word down the line that we are here to assist you and to unnerve the Fomorian. We will fly on ahead and confuse the Fomorian plans until you get there. Goodbye and good luck my friend."

With that the crow returned to the others above, and the black cloud passed over north eastwards at great speed and was quickly gone from view.

Niamh returned to the leading group and told the King what Seán Dubh had said and word was passed back until all the men were filled with confidence, so much so that groups of soldiers spontaneously burst out into song. Spirits were high and the mood positive, even the leading group were singing songs of old, songs of heroes and great acts of bravery.

The march continued without letup and as the leading group came over a rise, the coast and the great sea of Alba could be clearly seen.

"Rest the men here, eat and drink a little for in two hours we engage the Fomorian," snapped the High King.

The other Kings rode off down the lines passing the orders to the Captains as they went.

The great Gael army went silent as each warrior ate, drank and turned his thoughts inward to wives, sons, daughters and mothers and fathers. Most of the soldiers were related and there were fathers and sons, brothers and cousins here, here on this great day, a day that will be remembered for all eternity. They looked across at each other's faces, taking in every line and tiny blemish as if afraid they may forget. Some lay back on the grass and looked up at the sky, their mouths moving in silent prayer, others moved around nervously checking and rechecking their equipment.

Niamh walked down through the lines of soldiers, speaking to them and occasionally touching them as is the custom of a Priestess passing on the blessing of the Goddess. Niamh the girl was now a woman, a woman touched by the Goddess and the men responded by showing her great reverence. It is hard to think that only a few days ago she was an unknown junior Priestess of Brighde, now she is an instrument of the Mother Goddess Danu herself, and has the respect of Kings and commoners alike.

The two hours passed very quickly and very soon the men were battle readied and were marching in columns over the rise and towards the beach. The short distance was covered quickly and the Captains lead their men in ordered lines along the coastline a short distance from the water's edge. The noise of the sea and the crowing of the birds filled the air with expectation. The High King moved forward on his horse to within fifty paces of the water's edge and scanned the scene. A few unfinished Fomorian buildings sat on the sand.

"The weather had done its job," thought the King.

Out to sea the waters appeared fairly calm as there was no sign of any activity, just the occasional break of a wave on the shoreline. The King sat there looking intensely out to sea for several minutes before turning and giving orders for the men to stand down but remain vigilant.

The Fomorians

The End Game

With weapons and shields lowered, the extended line of Gael warriors stood transfixed looking out to sea. They didn't have to wait very long. One by one the Fomorian army began emerging from under the water until there was literally thousands of them standing up to their chests in the cool waters of the Sea of Alba. The Gaels quickly took up a defensive line, with shields raised and weapons at the ready. The King steadied his horse and moved back up the narrow beach towards his own line, and waited for the Fomorian to make the next move.

Suddenly a breeze began to blow and there was a definite change in the air. The sky was losing its other-worldly colour and the temperature was dropping. The High King ordered his men to be ready for now was the appointed time, destiny's time.

The Fomorian army started to move forward toward the beach, encouraged by the cooling air. They got to within twenty paces of the beach and stopped.

Conn ordered his men to stand firm.

"What are they waiting for?" he asked himself quietly.

The words were no sooner out of his mouth when a large man, dressed in black, pushed his way through the standing Fomorian army to the fore. He stopped in front of the first Fomorian and looked up at the clearing sky. The air temperature was now favouring the sea dwellers and he knew it. The Fomorian army now began to move forward.

The Gaels watched them with curiosity, for the legends say that the Fomorian was a race of ugly brutish giants, and they gained confidence in the knowledge that that was an exaggeration for these men were big, but not giants.

"Fall back to the sand dunes," ordered the King, and the men of the Gael began to step backwards in formation, maintaining their defensive shape.

A large gap had now been created between the two opposing armies with the Gaels occupying the high ground of the dunes, whereas, the Fomorian stopped and rearranged themselves into an attack formation. The man in black was busily giving orders and hardly noticed that a small young woman had pushed through the lines of the Gael and was moving down in the direction of the shoreline.

"Ah! What have we here, a gift from the King perhaps," spat the man in black after he had turned and noticed her standing there.

"I take it you are Francach?" asked the Priestess.

"Who is asking?" retorted the man in black.

"My name is Niamh, Priestess of the Goddess," she answered confidently.

"So the King sends a girl to fight his battles, does he?" Sneered the warrior, "and yes, my name is Francach, leader of the Fomorian army and soon to be High King of all Éirinn."

Then he let out a long burst of mocking laughter.

The Fomorians in the front ranks who could hear him all burst into spontaneous laughter.

Suddenly, all went quiet as Francach inched his way forward, and with a steely glare and malice in his voice he spoke again.

"Shall I slice off your head now and send it back to Conn, or shall we stand here all day passing pleasantries."

Niamh stood her ground and never flinched.

"Your sister Mòr is dead," she called out.

Francach stopped in his tracks.

"What?"

"Mòr is dead," Niamh repeated. "If you don't call off this invasion Francach, you will be joining her in the halls of your ancestors."

"Oh, and I suppose you child are going to stop me?"

Francach was now becoming very agitated with this brave, but seemingly stupid young woman. He reached behind into his belt and drew a small knife and hurled it at Niamh. The knife struck Niamh in the chest but she didn't fall as expected. "Forward!" He called as he drew his sword, but is men of the Fomorian army stood still watching the young Priestess standing on the sand with a dagger embedded in her chest.

"Forward I said," Francach screamed at the top of his voice, but he men still didn't move.

"Okay! I'll cut off her head and then perhaps we can get on with this," spat Francach.

King Conn was watching all of this unfolding before him, and just as he was about to give the order to rescue the Priestess a woman's voice interrupted.

"Let my Priestess deal with Francach, Conn High King of the Gaels."

Conn was so shocked at the unexpected voice of a woman on a potential battle field that he nearly fell from his horse. He quickly brought his horse under control and looked down to see a small woman standing there holding onto the horses bridle.

The small woman was looking intensely at what was happening on the beach not even raising her head to acknowledge if the King was hurt.

"Madam, what are you doing here, don't you know that we are squaring up to fight a battle. Leave at once or you may get injured."

"Your father said the very same to me many years ago at the ring of stones on Summer Solstice," She chuckled.

"Lady, I knew you would come," came a voice from behind them.

The King turned and saw Lulach down on one knee, with his head bowed.

Before the King could utter another word, the woman threw back her hood and revealed her identity.

"Ah! My trusty Bard, it is so good to see you again," said the lady.

Lulach stood up and looked up towards the King. "My Lord King Conn of Éirinn may I introduce the Goddess Danu."

The King sat on his horse with his mouth open, completely lost for words.

"I'm sure you will have plenty to say later" dismissed the Goddess, and once again turned her attention to the beach.

Francach looked at the priestess with his knife sticking out of her chest and sneered.

"Perhaps she's dead and hasn't fallen over yet, a little push and she'll go over like the corpse she is."

He extended his hand out to push her over but quickly withdrew as a searing pain shot through his hand. The man in black jumped back and pulled off his glove to find that the tops of two of his fingers were missing. Francach looked back to find that his army had not moved a muscle.

"Come on," he screamed, and then ran into the water to the first line of Fomorian warriors.

"What trickery is this?" his voice quaking with panic.

His army had been turned to stone and from the dunes and cliff tops looked like a giant road running out into the sea.

Francach now found himself alone, and he fell at the feet of the Priestess with his head bowed low. He looked around at the mighty army of the Gael gathered on the dunes and saw the hopelessness of his resistance.

"Priestess, I'm sorry for hurting you," he whimpered. His eyes were darting to and fro, looking for a possible escape route.

"The sea, the sea," he thought. "I will flee back into the sea and hide until my opportunity comes again."

"I didn't really mean you any harm," he lied, grovelling in the sand.

The Priestesses face was now glowing bright silver and as the daylight was beginning to fade a little, she shone like a star against the velvet night sky.

On top of the dunes the army of Gaels had all removed their helmets in reverence at what was unfolding before them. No one dared look away for fear of missing something important.

The Priestess glowed even brighter as her arms began to raise. There for all to see was a vision that no one would ever forget, for through the blinding silver glow could clearly be seen the triple aspects of the Goddess, Maiden, Mother and Wise Woman.

Francach could see that this was his chance as all the army were in awe of the vision before them and their attention had been drawn away from him.

With sword still in hand he looked up at the shining Priestess standing before him and moved quickly. He thrust the sword up into the belly of the Priestess and turned to run. Without looking back he ran at full speed into the sea and began to wade out into deeper water. It was then that he felt a pain. Every living thing that resides in the sea was attacking him, down to the smallest creature. Within seconds he was writhing about as his flesh was being stripped from his bones. His demise lasted only a short time.

Over time the sea itself dissolved his bones and Francach's life force returned to Tir-Nan-Og, the halls of his ancestors.

Down on the beach the Priestess stood shining like the moon on a clear night. She had a sword in her belly and a dagger in her chest. The High King, Drostan, Mordag and Lulach raced down to where she suspended and looked on in horror.

"Is she dead?" wept Mordag with tears streaming down her face.

"I guess she is," answered the King.

"Tut, tut, you Gaels, when are you going to believe," said a small voice from behind the glowing Priestess.

"Ah! Yes," stuttered the King clearing his throat. "It's not that we don't believe, we're just cautious by nature."

The Goddess looked at him and laughed, in fact everybody nervously laughed including the King himself.

The laughter ceased with a throat clearing cough as quickly as it had begun as the Goddess Danu walked around the glowing figure of Niamh.

"Well, we have two outcomes," continued the Goddess. "She can join me now in the realm of the Sidhe, or you can have her back and I'll take her later. Niamh is special, and she believes in the old ways, she will come to us of her own free will one day whatever you choose."

Drostan pushed forward, "My lady, if she lives can she marry, and can she come into the realm of the Danann's?"

Danu was in the process of removing the sword and the dagger and placing her hands on the young Priestess as Drostan asked his questions.

"Drostan my young Prince, why don't you ask her yourself?" said the Goddess.

Fully recovered and having no recollection of her ordeal, the Priestess asked confusedly what was going on.

Mordag quickly pushed in, "Niamh, Niamh, Drostan wants to propose."

Niamh turned to Drostan and asked, "To whom?"

"You, of course Niamh, will you marry me?"

"Well, like in all good stories Niamh married Drostan and Mordag fell in love with a handsome young Captain of the Danann guard. They all returned to the Village of the Salmon and were married by Lulach who had been made a Chief Druid of the Silver Branch by the Goddess herself, and three days later, after much merrymaking, they all returned beyond the veil into the land of the Danann's. Of course, time is different there and from time to time, the 'Wave Cutter' with its gossamer sails glides its way up the estuary and visits the world of men. Danu as is normal for Gods and Goddesses disappeared back into the

Sidhe realm and probably won't be seen for a very long time, but who knows? On long dark nights I think I've seen her passing through the land in her travelling guise as a fox, and if you keep your wits about you may see her too.

Those Fomorian soldiers, you know the ones from the battle, they are still there in the sea, and I reckon they'll be there forever, funny really; we call them the Giants Causeway, but I don't know if the name will stick. What do you think?

All I am sure of is this, never again will the peoples of Éirinn face each other in battle and peace will cover the land for a very long time. Well, I think it's time I went out and fed the birds, don't you? When all is said and done, we owe them a great deal and the one thing I've learned from this is that you never forget your friends."

The End

Pronunciations – Names & Places

Aodh = Hugh

Banbha = Ban-vah

Ban-Dubh = Ban-Doov

Branan = Bran-an

Brighde = Breed

Brugh Na Bóinne = Broo-na-boyn (New Grange)

Caiseal = Cash-el (Castle)

Cathal = Kat-al

Ceana = Kee-na

Ciaran = Kear-ran

Coinneach = Kenneth

Donnan = Doh-nan

Éirinn = Air-in (Ireland)

Eóghann = You-an

Fearghas = Fergus

Fionn = Fin

Fionntan = Fin-tan

Francach = Fran-kak

Gabhran – Gav-ran

Lulach = Loo-lak

Mòr = More

Morag = Mòr-ag

Mordag = Mòr-dag

Niall = Nile

Niamh = Neeve

Oenghus Mac Og = Angus Mac Og

Oisian = O-sheen

Orla = Awl-la

Raven = Rayven

Ròidh = Roy

Rónan = Roh-nan

Seán-Dubh = Shaun-doov
Sionn = Shaun (meaning Fox)
Sorcha = Shork-eh
Taran = Tar-ran
Teamhair = Tara
Una = Oona

Many thanks must be given to Nina Falaise for her wonderful Artwork and to Caiseal Mor for encouraging me to write this book.